XOW to SUCCEED IN ANESTXESIA SCXOOL

(And RN, PA, or Med Scxool)

NICK ANGELIS, CRNA, MSN

How to Succeed in Anesthesia School by Nick Angelis

© 2012, 2015, 2018 GG Press
In Association With

Print Edition License Notes

This book is dedicated to every student who felt that awful feeling of failure in the pit of their stomach but went back to clinicals anyway.

Table of Contents

Fiction Books by Nick Angelis:

Nonsense
Read Local
Christian Skits & Such
The Twerk Vaccine

Foreward by Anita Lesko

I was honored when Nick Angelis invited me to write the Foreword for his book *How To Succeed in Anesthesia School* for numerous reasons! First, I am a Certified Registered Nurse Anesthetist and have been working full time since graduating from Columbia University in New York City in 1988. Nick is pretty bizarre, but I've got him beat by a long-shot! Really! And I can prove it....I've got a certificate which states that I have Asperger's Syndrome! Best part of it though, is that I didn't know what Asperger's was until four years ago. As luck would have it, a co-worker's son was diagnosed with it. Lisa, also a CRNA, came to tell me of Gavin's diagnosis, presenting me with literature on Asperger's Syndrome. It was that moment when reading the 12 Cardinal signs of Asperger's, that I suddenly realized the mystery of my entire life-why I was so different, why I never fit in. I then wrote a memoir, *ASPERGER'S SYNDROME: When Life Hands You Lemons, Make Lemonade* and have been writing ever since.

So twenty nine years into it as a CRNA, over 50,000 cases to date, and over 1 million social interactions later, here I am writing this Foreword! When Nick sent me his manuscript to read, I experienced many laughing spells. Nick has an extremely dry sense of humor as I do, and that's how he writes it. Nick pretty much tells it like it is. Which actually is how us Aspies do it. In fact, at times I think Nick just might be an Aspie, but if not, he sure displays tendencies to qualify! Can I dare mention that I enjoy seeing Nick wandering around the lounge area with his hard-boiled egg in one hand, quietly obsessed with picking off the shell with the other, totally absorbed into the whole art of consuming a hard-boiled egg. I've decided that when Nick is deep in thought, he's pondering the mysteries of the universe, the theory of Relativity, or some such phenomenon. Nick is deep. And so is his book!

If you were not lucky enough to have been born with a dry sense of humor, you may find Nick's book confusing. Try to think out of the box. You should be doing that already. Life is really boring otherwise. But just in case it takes you awhile into the book to figure out Nick's obsession with sarcasm, be prepared for some bombshells he drops! I don't want to spoil the suspense. No one worth their salt ever tells the end of a movie or book, so don't expect it from me! You must experience Nick's drama as it unfolds!

I had an extremely rough time in both nursing and anesthesia school, because of my Asperger's syndrome that I didn't know I had! Everyone struggles in an intense training program like this, but for some even more so. Nick's various descriptions of crashing and burning might scare you, but don't dwell on it. He's giving examples of what can go wrong. None of us know what we're getting ourselves into when we sign up for it. It's sort of like a Trade Secret, that no one tells you what really happens! But yay for Nick! He presents the anesthesia student with a glimpse into this secret world of inducing people into comas! Remember that movie *Coma*? I can still see that image of lifeless-looking bodies floating......now I'm sounding weird like Nick. Are you laughing yet?

Nick's book will enable the reader, those interested in health care, to realize that there will be ups and downs during their reign as a student, but to keep persevering towards that final goal of graduating and joining the work force, hopefully as one of us elite anesthesia providers. Nick's wisdom and insight are invaluable, and give us all hope for the human spirit. One thing for sure....you will not fall asleep while reading Nick's book!

He has over fifteen years experience in healthcare, including some ridiculously awesome and occasional blood-curdling times. The best part is that this book only costs the equivalent of a few packages of Ramen noodles! You really get a bang for your buck with topics such as selecting a healthcare specialty, interviewing well, clinical tips, and how to react to accolades and failure even as a seasoned clinician. Starting at the "About the Author" section, this extended edition also contains an audio version of the book and *hidden bonus sections* (only Nick).

In closing, I hope I have convinced you this book will be an adventure and also helpful, providing you with insight into becoming a CRNA or one of the many other type of health professionals Nick mentions in this book. I would like to take this opportunity to wish you well on your journey into your new career and life.

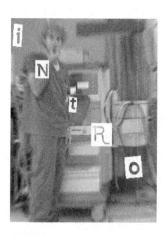

Introduction

   This book started with the much darker title "How to Screw up a Career in Healthcare." My coworkers pointed out that even the most enlightened reader may need a few chapters to understand my off-the-wall and occasionally pessimistic personality, hence the more encouraging title to this book. Despite the fact that I stole a balloon at the age of five, I've not lived a particularly remarkable life, so this book is not a biography. I couldn't even inflate the dumb thing because I didn't have the understanding of lung functional residual capacity (FRC) and expiratory volumes that I do now as a nurse anesthetist.

If you picked up this book because you want to get into anesthesia school but have no idea what I just said, put this book down and buy a physiology textbook instead. Read the chapter about the two balloony things in your chest. For everyone else, don't worry about it. This is a wittier book and a much better deal than the equivalent for getting into the pharmacy school or residency program of your dreams. My older brother says I'm full of nonsense for trying to apply what I've learned in nursing and anesthesia school to physician assistant, nurse practitioner, and similar career paths. But you see, I didn't write this book to explain how to squeak your way into the aforementioned school of your dreams. That's stupid in a clinical program. Your goal is to be an expert clinician at every stop in the path to your personal terminal degree. A terminal degree is usually a doctorate, but I interpret it as a place of contentment and fulfillment in your career choice.

Speaking of interpretation, I've endeavored to make this book as succinct and conversational as possible—though that probably means I should have used the word "tried" instead of "endeavored" and "short" instead of succinct. I reserve the right to waste your time with funny jokes and stories, but I've kept citations to a minimum other than linking them in the text. If you chase after every hyperlinked resource, you'll get sucked into an Internet wormhole of cat videos and medical memes, so I suggest ignoring links until you've at least finished the six chapters that mark the end of the first version of this book. Plus, you're holding the paperback version, so no matter how many times you've tapped underlined text, it still won't load a web page. I've kept a few links underlined so you know what to type into Google, and also to frustrate you. Thirsting for more? You can always email me for supplemental research to back up my prattling, and I'll be happy to set your academic heart aflutter or a. fib with scholastic ecstasy. I'll also email you a free .pdf/iBook/etc. version if you want, but the Kindle version should be cheaper if you bought this paperback.

With the exception of Twinkies and Big Macs, anything that stops growing turns stagnant and dies. This book, especially with the updates I've made for 2019, is not just for students. So many articulate, skilled clinicians never address and process their experience as students or their time at terrible jobs, especially if it was a toxic and frustrating period of life. They may appear well adjusted, only to destroy wealth or wreck their relationships years later. Let's get over it, but by going through the darkness and processing it directly instead of burying the ugliness. I don't believe that disease is just unexpressed emotions, or in the victim mentality that nurses and coddles hurts rather than moving on, but a common consequence is distorted self worth.

I don't want you to just experience success in your first job, but for an entire career working for hospitals, transitioning to locum tenens (similar to a nurse traveler) or finding contentment in a quiet office setting. None of this can happen if your identity as a person is tied to your performance as a clinician. That is why prestigious surgeons, RNs, or CRNAs can suddenly transform from poised adults to screaming children if something goes wrong. So what if you had to call for backup to successfully place a difficult nerve block? Ok, so we've seen bratty behavior the most from surgeons, because they can get away with it easier, but much like televangelist theology, a system that preaches that you are skilled and valuable and everything will work out only lasts until something wrong or unfair happens in life.

Back when I titled this book "How to Screw Up", I saw a void in the literature (and in disgustingly cheerful and unrealistic self help books) for those crucial years of schooling spent marrying the theoretical and clinical aspects of health care. It's not a pretty marriage at all. Patients rarely read the textbooks about the symptoms they should have and the clear disease processes they must exhibit to receive accurate diagnoses. Plus, many syndromes we treat at a superficial level to make symptoms bearable rather than address the root cause. It takes a lot more work and individualized care to trace a portion of a patient's chronic pain to inflammation from an unhealthy gut, or anxiety to a cortisol imbalance, than to just give the standard medicine and move on to the next patient. A skilled clinician is not the anesthetist who accurately treats the 90% of patients who respond normally to treatment, but one who can change the complex patient's story of, "Local anesthesia/nausea medicine/pain medicine/emotional support never works on me."

The earlier you can start planning your scholastic adventures, the easier the learning process to excel when challenged will be, so I've started at the very beginning: the first hint that listening to the complaints of cantankerous patients and exponentially increasing your exposure to harmful and exotic microorganisms might be the lifestyle for you. Although still focusing on succeeding in graduate school, this book arcs from making your first career choices in healthcare to the goal that my younger brother set for me as an agency nurse hustling for work (more on that later) and now as a CRNA: "Don't kill anyone."

Planning for Success

"Show fear on your face," I thought to myself as I raced down the hospital hallway as fast as my hideous white nursing shoes could take me. I could hear my nurse preceptor breathing heavily a few steps behind me. Any second and the gastroenterologist would cut a hole into the abdomen of my patient to place a feeding tube. Any second and she could bleed to death from the anticoagulant I accidentally switched for her routine antibiotic.

We finally reached the procedure area, where a preoperative nurse was staring at the empty IV bag of Argatroban hanging over my patient where Vancomycin should have been.

"Stop!" My preceptor yelled, and broke down in tears. I felt terrible but could only manage to wrinkle my face into a disheartened frown. Sometimes being the calm one had its disadvantages. The patient was fine, but I couldn't help thinking,

"I'm two months into my first job as a registered nurse. How am I going to make it in anesthesia school if I'm such a moron?"

It was a fair question. This isn't a book to reassure you that if you try hard enough, you can do anything. Maybe you can't, and no one is willing to sacrifice patient safety to give a nitwit the luxury of repetitive do-overs. Nor should they: hard results matter, such as whether the patient lived or died and if your care contributed to one of those outcomes. That's why this book isn't structured like a cheery motivational speech. Trite sayings won't help you. After all, if you aim for the moon but miss and land among the stars, the sun's corona has a habit of vaporizing dreams at several million degrees Fahrenheit. Actually, I take back my opinion of cheesy sayings. There is a relevant quotation by Albert Einstein: "Insanity is doing the same thing over and over and expecting different results."

That's why it's so important to learn your own strengths and weaknesses as a person before you ever become a clinician. We do this in every other aspect in life. If you have the extremity strength of a new-born fawn, it's unwise to challenge your date to an arm wrestling competition, and if you're a terrible guesser, Rock Paper Scissors is a dangerous game. I was going to say "upper extremity strength of a T-Rex", but let's save that joke for later, because a T-Rex is still going to beat me at arm wrestling, meat eating, and generally looking awesome all day long. What skills do you have now that people will pay you to do? What did you want to be when you grew up? I wanted to be a clown until I realized that they had weak unions and circus life didn't come with good benefits (this was around the same time that I stole that FRC emptying balloon). Since I was good at science and a few useless creative skills like acting (and hopefully writing), I applied my abilities to nursing school. My ultimate goal of becoming a certified registered nurse anesthetist took a hit when I realized that anesthesia schools demand fifty to eighty hours a week year round, with maybe two weeks off a year if you're lucky. Incidentally, those acting skills help me keep a straight face in a culture that is more similar to the show "Scrubs" than "ER."

You're probably wondering why I'm already straying off topic a few pages into this book, especially since the introduction specifically states that this book isn't a biography. The "Scrubs" vs. "ER" mentality is a valid point however, because you need to plan for success socially in a rigid world where respect often depends on the initials following the name on your ID badge. The weird story I began this chapter with was really about me realizing I needed to shed my Spock-like demeanor for a more distraught one, given the circumstances and despite the freaking out I was already doing on the inside. Transfer the effort it takes to appear serene into changing the outcome. Dull and boring personalities can be just as successful as sparkling ones, so there's no need to resign yourself to counting pills in the back of a cramped drug store or cheering up pediatric cancer patients with your sunny disposition and charming smile. There are certainly traits and attitudes that will increase your chances at success as a student, but we'll discuss those in the appropriate chapters.

For many people, even in healthcare, social times outside of work just aren't possible without enough alcohol to enjoy the presence of your coworkers. Plan to control addictions before you start, as all of the careers listed on the title of this book are full time, life-consuming endeavors. A temporary addiction to ramen noodles during school may be unavoidable, but the key is to stay as healthy and clear-headed as possible. Remembering priorities and your weaknesses is crucial to avoid distractions. Unless you're not working hard enough, your relationships will undergo strain. One anesthesia school that interviewed me revealed they had a 33% divorce rate among their students. I've updated the back of the book with a section on relationships because this sensitive topic needs to be honestly addressed. Again, inane encouragement and perseverance is relatively useless, much like a T-Rex trying to compensate for the obvious with really muscular thighs, or substituting hope for knowledge. You might not emerge from school with a white head of hair like a president leaving the White House (maybe Trump's skin will turn more orange from the stress?), but you may pick up a few pounds or a greater dependence on caffeine—if not nicotine or alcohol—before you're done. Of course, a Starbucks addiction would probably have helped me stay awake more often in nursing and anesthesia classes!

Talking about caffeine brings up one of the most important topics in this book, although it has nothing to do with healthcare. At what point should you start denying yourself the simple pleasures of four dollar coffee or blowing a hundred bucks every weekend? When do you really need to start saving? The truth is, it could take decades to dig yourself out of debt if you don't take the necessary steps now. There is absolutely no point in putting yourself and your loved ones through years of essentially monastic living if you'll still be living paycheck to paycheck with a higher salary once you graduate. I can speak with authority on this subject, because I never took out a student loan and had enough capital after anesthesia school to afford the down payment on a house.

Of course, in order to avoid loans, I spent several years working seventy hours a week, so let's begin with a more practical approach: interest rates. As I'm writing this book, student loans are at such low rates that financing your life with them (and skipping the next few rambling paragraphs) is a viable option. I previously recommended that students pay off their undergraduate loans before starting graduate school, but it's an individual decision and also depends on the degree you are pursuing. Transferring loans from one 0% interest credit card to another works until you make a single mistake. Risking money you need for next semester's tuition or next week's canned soup is a bad idea once you're in school, on par with investing all your money in foreign stock the day before you retire. Some research on your part is necessary to avoid investing in the "Anesthesia Student Wire Transfer Fund of Northwest Potiskum". I've included a separate section and my own exclusive, peer-reviewed research on investing for healthcare folk in the last chapter.

As much as it depends on you, keep your other debts to a minimum. For example, don't make illegitimate children—child support really adds up. Chronic illnesses tend to be expensive too, although avoiding carcinogens may be more difficult than wearing seatbelts, selling your motorcycle, or resisting the urge to sled down an icy hill on a skateboard. The last time I had such an urge, I at least had the presence of mind to increase my life and disability insurance first—which is a must if you have a family, once you do reach your terminal degree.

If you have a GPA above 3.0 or an interesting characteristic (e.g. Navajo and Guatemalan heritage), the first step is to look for scholarships and grants. Regardless of the angle I tried in high school, no one accepted my Greekness as any race or ethnicity other than Dark White. My GPA and essay skills were good enough to justify the time I spent submitting scholarship applications instead of working at "Niko's House of Gyro and Lamb". There really is no such place in my hometown, but if there were, I'd eat there twice a week.

To be honest, all my scholarships combined were laughable had I gone anywhere but the local public university. Getting involved as a commuter student led to more scholarship opportunities once I was enrolled. The prestige of your alma mater is at best a tiny variable for your success in healthcare. This isn't business school, where networking is more important than what you learn. I had friends who finished accelerated premed degrees at my humble undergrad institution so they could start medical school early and pay off their debt faster. Even for your terminal degree, selecting a more prestigious school with a more expensive price tag is rarely worth it. One possible exception exists if MD or PA are the initials you want to follow your name; it's harder to graduate with your first degree in four years because of limited class availability at a community college or public university.

Saving money requires making money. You can thank me later for the novel ideas expressed in this book. Healthcare experience is great, but so is not going bankrupt. An entry level healthcare job doesn't have to be permanent, especially since you need to put yourself in the best financial health possible. I have a friend in Physician Assistant school whose first job as a hairdresser makes her surgical clinicals much easier than for her colleagues who don't have the hand dexterity she learned using scissors and razors all day. However, hands-on health care experience is invaluable, especially for PAs, AAs, and MDs. Otherwise, your first real clinical experience will be at the graduate level. That's a little late to notice that you don't like hospitals because they smell weird. I mean, maybe three months at a nursing home is all you need to polish the skills of irrational patient (and rashy patient) management. From there you can move on to a higher paying job until you finish your undergraduate degree. Who knows? Maybe some of your scruffy-looking classmates will need highlights and a trim from you before an important interview.

Despite my encouragement, the usefulness of a "bottom of the totem pole" job in healthcare depends on the type of person you are. On a more general level, if you're an arrogant jerk, the experience might increase the empathy for patients and coworkers we all could use more of. The more broken you are emotionally ("soul wounds" is one trendy term to describe spiritual and psychological hindrances that must be worked through), the more difficult it becomes to deeply understand what someone else is going through. For me personally, I'm easily contented, and I didn't realize that my job as a nurse tech was horrible until I became a nurse. I learned about involving patients in their care in nursing school, so as a tech on an orthopedic floor, I asked patients how I could best help them maneuver after surgery. One day as I was wrenching my back in a futile attempt to move a rather unmotivated patient, a cynical possibility came to me. Maybe these patients didn't have a clue how to best move around—maybe that's why they'd fallen and broken their various bones in the first place.

Years later, a much more useful job for me was that of an agency nurse, the healthcare equivalent of a substitute teacher. I often negotiated my own contracts, and soon realized that many of the nurses complained the same whether they had an easy job or a hard one. They hadn't compared other places to know the difference, and in some cases had taken their manager's word for it. Sometimes the grass is greener on the other side, but it takes more than a glance to find out.

I have to admit that it was mostly my fault that I didn't get much out of my first healthcare job. I had a 4.0 in college but very little common sense. One of my professors tried to explain it this way,

"Common sense tells you that 100 units of insulin is too much!"

The perpetrator in that case actually did have common sense. If you think about my professor's comment, common sense doesn't tell you anything about arbitrary doses of medicine. What I lacked was the intuitive knowledge of how to be useful. I would finish a task and try to take the initiative to do the next needed thing, but it didn't come nearly as naturally for me as knowing the indications and dosages for a variety of insulins. Until I took that first job, I didn't realize that my strength in "book smarts" was beyond many graduated nurses and my weakness in seeing the whole picture was equal to a sub-par waiter at Denny's. One solution for me was shadowing. When it was my turn to visit the OR in nursing school, I spent my time with a nurse anesthetist to see what I needed to work on. All the research you can do about a career won't be as useful as seeing for yourself what that person does. I also wanted to know if the CRNA lifestyle fit with mine. For a quick example, a nurse practitioner or physician assistant working for an orthopedic surgeon usually won't have reliable work hours unless patients agree to only fracture their hips from nine to five. Signing a release guaranteeing all pelvic and femur bone fragments to line up appropriately for ninety minute surgeries would also be helpful.

Even a few months as a tech or aid under the whims of, to borrow a few stereotypes, menopausally challenged nurses or boring pharmacists may be all you can stand. You can only "shadow" so many professions while on the job before becoming the company creeper, and if you're a more hands on learner you may want to fall back on a better paying job if preparing for a long academic road. A friend of mine still works part time as a firefighter because of the health insurance and pension plan, while another nurse I know works at an upscale restaurant on the weekends because his large tips equal the money he'd making working those hours as a nurse.

I don't intend to imply that jobs in healthcare pay poorly until you have a bachelor's degree or beyond. Many of my fellow nurse anesthetists started as paramedics, radiology technicians, and similar occupations before becoming ICU nurses and applying for anesthesia school. In fact, you can spend your entire working career at one institution, using tuition reimbursement programs each step of the way as your education and paychecks increase. This method never appealed to me because I knew exactly where I wanted to go and didn't have any debt. I tried using tuition scholarships from my various places of employment, but I always barely missed qualifying because of some technicality or other. There are some great options, though. As of my writing, Amazon just announced that their fulfillment center employees are eligible for 95% of their education paid for after three years of employment.

If you do choose to take your career slowly and advance each time you qualify for more tuition reimbursement, but find something you love along the way to your goal, there's no shame in stopping. Few people in American culture have a concrete idea of exactly how much money is enough. We Greeks, on the other hand, as soon as we figure out the weekly cost of baklava, flaming cheese, and coffee—wait, that's a bad comparison, forget I mentioned it. A classic example is a nurse with a diploma or associate degree. Unless you want to become a professor or advanced clinician, there's inadequate financial or academic reward for that next step. Most nurses disagree with me on that, and a good opposing opinion can be found in my friend Kati Kleber's book, *What's Next? The Smart Nurse's Guide to Your Dream Job.* I've written extensively on her FreshRN and FreshNP blogs and barely resisted the urge to copy/paste those posts into this book, because that's lame. Anyway, the love of learning may dim when it contributes to your debt but not your paycheck! Of course, the knowledge I gained from RN to CRNA was similar in magnitude to what I gained from telemarketer to RN. When I learned anesthesia, I was embarrassed by the arrogance I had as a nurse, thinking I knew how drugs worked.

Most colleges offer free career surveys to discover how much learning, prestige, and salary really matter to you in your occupation. Studies show that a plumber can make as much money as a doctor when taking debt into account, but acquiring your terminal degree at a trade school means you have to be smart with your money since you'll accumulate it slower. As a conscientious reader, you're probably hoping I've cited the plumber/doctor study at the end of this chapter so you can peruse it later. I haven't. A little internet searching will be good for honing those academic sleuthing skills. Back to tech and entry level positions, changing jobs is also easier at this level, but you have to know how much personal fulfillment and independence you want with the job. It's expensive to have three or four totally different degrees that you're not using. The surgeons I work with making millions of dollars complain about bills just like everyone else, so have a concrete idea of what level of income you need. For example, a sugar momma I worked with as an agency nurse wouldn't have had to work so many hours if she wasn't also supporting her eighteen year old boyfriend's weed habit. (I tried to teach her negotiation skills, but nurses buying illegal drugs don't have much leverage). You slave in school so you don't have to slave for the rest of your life.

Remember that highly specific tech and medical sales jobs pay well but may require travel or relocation. Plus, there's a higher possibility of the role not being future proof—just ask all those unemployed bloodletters. It's much harder to make money selling Lipitor now that many cholesterol drugs are generic and modern science is finally realizing the potential shortsightedness of the anti-fat campaign. In the case of specialized tech jobs, they may have little relevance to your ultimate goal—monitoring brain impulses or running lithotripsy machines in an OR would be of little use to an office-based PA or a community-based clinical nurse specialist. Working with a bachelor's in nursing until you have the money (and experience) for anesthesia school is an example of the second method toward your career destination.

Nursing is more flexible but favors the approach of advancing through degrees slowly, hopefully paying off most loans between degrees. In the case of nurse clinician or practitioner schools, the debt is less of a factor since it's easier to work while in school, which is why some people decide to start graduate school as soon as they have a bachelor's degree. You can start as a licensed practical nurse (LPN—look, I defined an acronym for the first time!) or with an associate's degree in nursing and have a considerable amount of options. On the other hand, it's hard to translate your skills into similar occupations if you have a master's degree in anesthesia or perfusion! Other than teaching, your options are limited to a specific task in the OR.

The Interview Process

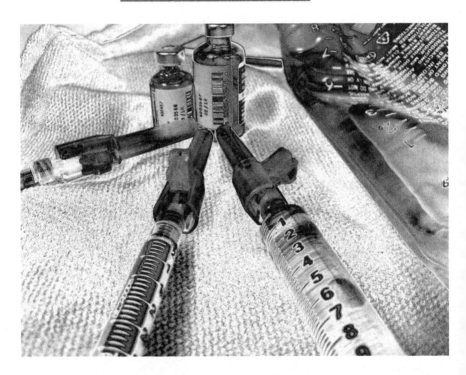

I expected to easily finish this book a few months ago, and here I am starting the second chapter. Getting into school is a similar process in that there's more work and time involved than you'd suppose. The worst thing you can do is procrastinate because of some vague requirement or elusive document that the school demands. No, you don't want to look needy and helpless (that secretary you keep calling is an important gatekeeper), but you certainly can't afford to miss deadlines and be pleading with professors who barely remember your name for effusive reference letters at the last minute. Do the legwork or move on to a school that doesn't require you to retake Geography of Middle Earth (yes, I have taken that class) before applying. It may be difficult not to let all of the requirements to hang over your head. Different schools have tasks to complete in order to grant an interview that vary in difficulty from faxing a resume to destroying a golden ring with addictive and invisible properties.

Don't let preparation for the next phase in your life cause you to miss the present. The worst attitude is "I can't learn anything from where I am right now, I can't wait until I'm a doctor, nurse, etc." Do you really want to be the pharmacist perplexed by the clinical environment in your last year of school, or the hapless nurse well-versed in Orem's theories but not any practical help on a hospital unit? Learn as much as you can every step of the way. Saving patient's lives often requires quick, irreversible decisions. First impressions in a health care environment are similar. We're wired to make snap judgments.

So, check for food in your teeth, dress in dark colored, conservative clothes, and wear deodorant the day of your interview. That's not to say that people are any meaner than normal in healthcare. In my hobo nurse—er, agency nurse days, I'd run into a new unit for the start of a seventy-five hour work week and clock in with seconds to spare. My next task would be to find the clean utility room where patient supplies are kept. I'd borrow a comb, mouthwash, and once in a while, some warm peri-wipes usually reserved for incontinent patients. Don't judge, I only used them in instances where I was playing basketball or at a crowded concert before I threw on my wrinkled scrubs and raced to work. What would your first impression be of a new coworker who smelled just like your patients? I received many strained, tight-lipped smiles.

Unless you're a CRNA and they're asleep, you can't tell your patients what you really think of them. That politeness almost transcends to coworker relationships, but often sticks somewhere between gossip and passive-aggressive behavior. My personal approach is to look really serious and say things like, "Cheetahs can only charge at 65mph for about a quarter mile, but the key is in the flexibility of their spine." The perpetrator gets unsettled trying to find the passive or aggressive meaning behind my nonsensical statement and leaves me alone. Forever. Other than by glazed looks of horror, no one ever told me directly not to act homeless on the job, but I'm sure I became an interesting topic of discussion.

Sometimes it can be difficult to discern the unwritten dos and don'ts of various healthcare settings, although I have reached the conclusion that personal use of patient wipes are a "don't". This is another advantage of immersing yourself in hospital culture before it matters. But isn't each facility and region different? Absolutely, and treatment of various conditions can differ despite standard treatment procedures. Again, going to school locally will help mitigate some of this, provided that you don't have a reputation as "the pharmacy tech who gave Mrs. Smith Lithium instead of Lasix." Find a graduate of the program you want to attend. I've been Facebooked often about anesthesia school by total strangers, and some of them were creepy. Especially at the graduate level or when considering different residency programs, experiences can be totally different from one place to another. Even a heads up on the way that a school interviews candidates can be useful, as long as it comes from a reliable source (i.e., not a scorned and bitter interviewee). Contacting people directly via LinkedIn or searching the forums on that site is probably a less intrusive way to find relevant information, but I'd caution you not to waste too much time searching for wisdom on the internet. You'll just find blathering fools, random haters, and people like me spewing unfair generalizations.

Start the process with what you have least control over—the previous example of begging people for reference letters is a good place. It's not unethical to give them a deadline weeks ahead of the actual deadline. Balance the expertise and relevance of your recommender with how well you know him or her and how well you've performed for them. If this will be your first career taking care of patients, schools will be a bit more focused on making sure you're not a psycho, so a personal reference about your character may be more valuable than one from a doctor who doesn't really know your name. Your life experiences and knowledge of the profession should also be strong points. The process itself of writing essays, preparing for exams, and fielding tough questions may help you guide your decisions as well. In my case, I gathered personal recommendations and documents to be awarded a scholarship covering room and board at my undergraduate university. The only task remaining was a 500 word essay on why I wanted to be a university scholar. I touched my pen to the paper and thought, "The cafeteria's chicken pizza tastes like popcorn," followed by, "If I write 500 words about why I want to get this scholarship to live on campus, 450 of them will be a lie."

Hopefully your decisions won't hinge on pizza quality, but thinking ahead is necessary. If your final goal is to be an NP, but you love your family and there are great CNS programs near you, don't move across the country for that random school that *US News & World Report* ranked so highly. I hope this won't come as a shock, but those rankings are meaningless. I could write a chapter on this topic alone, but suffice it to say that the statistics they and other ranking agencies use don't cover first time fail rates on qualifying exams or the all important attrition rates. That's one reason I often encourage members of the armed forces to advance their healthcare careers at a civilian school, where they won't have military regulations as an additional factor making it difficult to complete a degree.

There are nurse anesthesia schools that allow you to work by combining evening classes with flexible clinical schedules, though the schooling will take you longer. Online schools for a general MSN count your job as clinical hours, and nurse practitioner programs exist that will accept non-nurses if location isn't important to you. Manage an inopportune sidestep on your career path by finding a school with a bridge program, e.g. from PA to MD or ADN to MSN. "ADN" meaning an associate's degree in nursing—don't mistake that for "MLEA", My Laziness Exposed by Acronyms.

In contrast to searching out a school that fits your needs like a luer lock, another way to make life easier is attending a school locally or where you at least know people. Establishing a support system wherever you're going is important. Of course, I mean a positive support system. I was surprised when a program director asked me during an interview," How much alcohol do you drink a night?" I felt like my patients must when I ask them about "recreational drug use", as if powdered trails of crack were trickling out of their nostrils. Besides evaluating your critical thinking skills, interviewers might ask detailed questions about your financial situation, personality, and typical job interview topics. For instance, if you can't work at all during school, will you survive on credit cards, investing your saved money somewhere with reasonable interest rates (lendingclub.com is one option for investors and borrowers), or by praying weekly for anonymous checks to arrive in the mail? No one wants a student without a plan, so, "Where do you see yourself in five years" is bound to come up. Thankfully, you've read the first chapter already, so you should have an idea of your end goal.

Of course, what directors and professors *won't* want to hear is a radically different plan B and C in case the program interviewing you doesn't work out. It's ok to mention other schools offering the same degree you've applied to if asked. Many schools have $500 application fees, so it's unlikely that you'll have applied to six different schools and subsequently appear desperate. Some anesthesia schools provide a master's in health science or PhD in pharmacy instead of a master's or doctorate in nursing like most other nursing specialties. The same principle I mentioned with diploma and associate degree prepared registered nurses holds true. After a few years, no one can demonstrate statistics showing one degree to be safer than another, although the difference in debt is certainly significant! This is also true when comparing anesthesiologists, nurse anesthetists, and anesthesiology assistants. In case my opinion isn't clear, think of the last time you received a hair cut (perhaps by the PA student I mentioned earlier). What would you look at first, the certificates proclaiming barber education on the wall, or the haircut your stylist's last client just received? Chances are, you'll be going elsewhere if the last customer looks like they cut their hair in a blender, even if a certificate proclaiming a PhD in Follicular Management is hanging on the wall.

Your goal is not to find the easiest or the most challenging, but the best fit. A good website to contrast different anesthesia schools is all-crna-schools.com (although it's not completely accurate), and the AANA website can be a very valuable resource. Talking with people who work at main clinical sites or former graduates is the best way to learn what a school is really like. In the previous chapter, I mentioned that cost is a huge factor in healthcare education. Each school is credentialed to make sure they are teaching the same academic material, so it's unlikely that one program is really worth an extra $20,000 to attend. Instead of just searching for the most prestigious institution, you should focus on cost differences. Is there a separate fee paid to the clinical site? If a stipend exists, does it involve selling your soul for eternity? Quality matters. Will you be taught to the full extent of your profession's scope of practice at clinical sites, or will those sites just abuse you as free labor? Obviously, don't attend a school with credentialing issues or one that is under any sort of academic probation. This is more important in less mainstream fields (like the quest to receive a master's degree in alternative medicine), where a little research can reveal that a school is unaccredited by CHIA or another regional accrediting agency and therefore worth as much as a "health coach" certificate.

Criteria for selecting a school differ widely among professions. In a baccalaureate nursing program or even as a clinical nurse specialist, clinical sites have much less influence on your performance than they would in clinician-focused graduate schools. This is because you are expected to learn many of your clinical skills at your first job, which also means that selecting that first job will probably be more important than deciding on a particular school to attend. Contrast that with a chiropractor or, even better, a midwife— even as a new graduate, you need to know exactly what you're doing when that fetus wants to explore new horizons!

Back to the actual interview process, clinical questions about your specific field of study are becoming more common, although still less important than displaying expertise in whatever healthcare experience you've had thus far. If your ambition is anesthesia school, pay attention to how the anesthetists manage ICU patients when they transfer care after surgery, and learn everything you can about the top ten drugs they use. Occasionally work in the PACU and ER if your hospital has a float pool. Some of you are imagining serene nurses paddling happily, their hats bobbing with the lazy current of the float pool. Others suspect that the ebook version links to a hilarious Gomerblog about this meaningless topic. It's ok if you've never heard of many of the phrases I'm using in this chapter. Even if all you've done is transport patients or answer phones in a hospital, relaying how to work as a team or do your part if a patient takes a turn for the worse shows your capacity to learn. That's what every school or residency program looks for. GPA tells part of the story, as do the GRE or MCAT achievement tests. As acceptance into health care schools becomes more competitive, even entry level programs are incorporating interviews into the selection process— otherwise, previous GPA is the most important factor. The trend is also towards more substantive interviews, which is what you should look for in a program, unless you have horrible interview skills or a difficult-to-hide third hand.

I already mentioned that you shouldn't necessarily look for the most demanding programs, because you might graduate equally qualified as your peers from other schools, but much more tired. However, a challenging interview process, even if it includes a test and answering clinical questions similar to a medical oral exam, shows a school's commitment to the students they choose. Many schools are flexible in deciding how many students to admit each year, depending on the quality of applicants. Hopefully, this rigorous process allows the school to clinically and didactically support those they do select, because of how carefully program and clinical directors made their choices. Getting in should be the hardest part, not staying in. The weeding out process needs to take place before classes and clinicals start! In most nursing programs, for example, physiology and organic chemistry prerequisites quickly separate the wheat from the chaff.

As an aside, please don't misunderstand my explanation of what an ideal program should look like. You may decide to enter a nightmarish education because you've always wanted to be an anesthesiologist or clinical pharmacist and are unwilling to let anything to get in your way, even the sketchy schools in the Caribbean. And, no matter what your academic or clinical credentials are, there is no such thing as a guarantee. I almost typed "shoo-in", but have no desire to mimic the writing style of a middle-aged women you'd expect to see bobbing in a hospital float pool. Anyway, it's not uncommon for a program with a good reputation from previous graduates to snap up the more qualified students. If you simply aren't the best candidate or have been denied twice by other schools, you may end up at an overpriced or undervalued institution. Your success is completely up to you, just like Dwight Howard's will now that he has transferred his credentials from the lowly Orlando Magic to the more prestigious research institution commonly referred to as the Lakers. No one will accept the difference in coaching, training, or facilities as an acceptable excuse when it comes time to perform.

I assume you are hoping I will stop watching ESPN while writing this book and answer, "What other purposes does the interview serve?" In anesthesia school, it establishes expertise in your specialty. After learning that I was a cardiac surgery ICU nurse, an anesthesiologist interviewing me asked if doctors prescribed Digoxin in my ICU. I answered "yes", thinking that we did occasionally continue the drug if a patient was already on it, although our inotropic drug of choice was Milrinone. Unfortunately, the doctor didn't stop there but asked complex questions about IV loading doses and therapeutic levels. I can't tell you whether it'll sound like a cop out to mention that Digoxin is prescribed more often in the heart failure units of your facility. If your experience is from a very specific unit requiring intimate knowledge of a dozen drugs, you should expect more focused questions than if you worked in a more generalized ICU.

Interviews also allow programs to gauge common sense and the ability to think on your feet. These are vital skills and their absence is often cloaked by good essay writing or high test scores. With my background, good clinical sense translates into making sure pacer wires haven't disconnected if a heart monitor flatlines, or making sure that a low reading from a pulse oximeter isn't due to the monitor reading the bed sheet's oxygenation status instead of the patient's! It's the ability to quickly adapt, and schools investigate this skill to avoid filling the last few slots with students they suspect will struggle in the program, despite a stellar GPA or experience in a demanding clinical environment.

Universally, most interviews end with, "Are there any questions that you might have?" Don't be distracted or confused that I didn't update the 2012 edition of this book by talking about new Lakers player Lebron James instead of Dwight Howard. Should you waste this opportunity to ask if the clinical uniforms are scratchy or could pass as a 70's bowling team? You're not there to do standup. I can afford the risk of offending every ninth person I say something hilarious to, but you can't. Questions you should ask are "How well do you support your students once they are accepted?" and the corollary, "What is your attrition rate?" This type of questions work best in the context of future plans by showing that you're not blindly entering a field you know nothing about just because someone you know with a nice car is a physical therapist. Otherwise, you'll look scared. Find out what the process is for conflict resolution between clinical sites and the school. How supportive and involved is the school with clinical sites? This is not a deal breaker in the least, but medical schools differ widely in the support they give their students during rotations. A good question would be, "Will I need to personally find locations for my general and specialty rotations in the last two years of medical school?" It can be harder to land that dermatology rotation if you're cold calling clinics.

You might want to reword that last question so you don't sound plaintive or the "L" word. Unless you're dropkicking babies in the hospital parking lot again, there aren't many reputations worse for a student than being called lazy. Interviewing requires some political skill, but being yourself and showing willingness to work hard goes farther than appearing smooth and collected. Of course you'll be nervous, and you should be. Some transparency on your part will reduce the chance that your insightful questions and answers belay pessimism or arrogance.

Clinical Tips for Anesthesia School

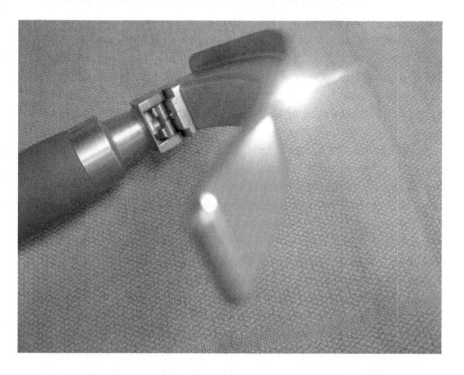

Except for this sentence, I've taken extra care not to write anything witty in this chapter to prevent feelings of being left out if you're not in anesthesia school and therefore skip to the next section. It goes without saying that all the legal disclaimers found in textbooks apply to this chapter. You know, the statement that medical science is quickly advancing, so trying something just because you read it in this book without consulting other sources is asinine. I mean, you did buy this off the internet after all, which is slightly less prestigious than calling in an order after watching an infomercial. The same disclaimer applies to the relationship and finance chapters—really, every sketchy sentence I've written. Some of the concepts here are easily transferable to other disciplines, but I've made no attempt to do so. The clinical nuances of advanced practice professions can be very specific, and it would be terrible if I both took your money and led you astray. And also hilarious, so don't tempt me.

Do you see how ugly the above picture is? Not the beautiful one of a Macintosh 4 laryngoscope about to access your airway; I am referring to the picture of a puke green, rusting metal cabinet with some pediatric equipment and weirdly-tinged propofol scattered on top of it. I probably didn't pay extra for color, so if all the pictures look gray, you're not color blind. Anesthesia school is not glamorous. Neither was your infomercial purchase last paragraph, but I'm glad that your bowels are already more regular. On the healthcare hierarchy totem pole, graduate students are still a bug trapped underneath the pole. Clinical days pass in some forgotten corner of a hospital basement watching a little kid sleep for hours with no chance for heroism in sight. One of my friends puts it this way, "The hardest part of my job is being tired and watching all these patients enjoy restful sleep all day." The take-off and landing are exciting, but the time in-between can be a strange mix of hyper arousal and boredom. I explain that mix as the continuum of vigilance in health care, with carelessness and laziness at one end and frantic fear at the other. The continuum explains many of the inevitable skirmishes you will have with your anesthesia preceptors.

Realize that all those clichés about stopped clocks being right twice a day apply here as well. If you meet a CRNA with a completely different perspective, don't be defensive or take things personally (even if they're meant that way), but don't accept abuse either. Instead, be paranoid with the paranoid. This profession attracts people with OCD tendencies, and if you don't appear meticulous they'll hover over you like a fat kid at a cookie party. If something goes suddenly and terribly wrong, it'll take more time to put away your smart phone or newspaper and fix the problem if the syringes and equipment are disorganized! Of course, in the name of organization, I once had an evil preceptor who informed me that my medication stickers were on the wrong side of the syringe. For the slower/partially anesthetized among you, syringes are cylinders, which are circles, which don't have sides. Don't feel bad, I once received a 0% on a Geometry quiz I spent an hour working on. Worst moment of eleventh grade right there. The best moment was taking a Barbie doll to Homecoming, but now you're distracting me. Identifying psychotic preceptors is an invaluable tool as an anesthesia student. My BEHAVE Wellness project on bullying and corporate wellness can help with some of this. Who can you trust? Programs with multiple clinical sites have a liaison between the school and the program, although that doesn't automatically mean anything. Find out from students who have been to that hospital before, although they may be more loyal to CRNAs at an institution than they will be to you. Seniors may be after a job or desperately want to please someone at the hospital with juicy information about a new student. At this point of the book, you may suspect I'm a suspicious sourpuss. I'm actually embarrassingly gullible and tend to see the best in people rather than their glaring faults and skewed perceptions, which is why advice like this was so helpful for me. And really, you should be treating everyone as well as you can. Not two-faced or disingenuous, but the way you want to be treated. The simpler you can keep your OR relationships, the better you can concentrate on doing well clinically instead of the petty drama that some people live for.

Once you do find preceptors that have your best, long-term interests in mind and really want to help you, try new things and work on your clinical weaknesses with them. As a new student, skills like arterial and intravenous line placement and intubating with a new type of blade or equipment are good examples. Even discovering your deficits may seem bewildering. One preceptor will compliment you on your critical thinking and the next may berate you for the exact same thought process. Understand that many of the brilliant anesthetists who ask highly specialized and difficult questions only have one or two areas of didactic expertise, unless they've been reading textbooks between cases. Often there's a strong correlation between a fixation with patient positioning or airway or narcotic dosing and a mistake they once made. Even if an outcome is one in a million, if it happens to your patient, you'll pay special attention to it in every subsequent case until you retire (or receive adequate therapy).

As a quick side note, would extensive counseling help you

survive and perhaps even thrive in anesthesia school? The answer is yes—one of the reviewers of this book, Elizabeth Scala, is a nurse and wellness coach, and my two CRNA colleagues and I who regularly write and speak about these topics counsel students often. The problem is that if you had the time and money for weekly counseling during school, you wouldn't really need it. The signs of exceeding capacity, such as inability to control emotions, will be present during this overwhelming season of life, but concentrate on reactions to stress more than the stress itself. Similar to training your brain how to study, resilience is one of the most important skills you should master. This is quite different than stubbornness, which can be evidenced clinically as trying a spinal for a sixth time instead of just changing that inflexible plan and performing general anesthesia. Later, we will talk much more about this and how to build a healthy, balanced support system that doesn't suck or suck your loved ones dry.

Coworkers, supervisors, and subordinates all follow the same rule: no one wants to work with those who make their job harder, even if they're attractive, funny, and show up early every day. I travel often thanks to the Witness Protection Agency (just kidding), and this point hits home when I rent my house to vacationers while I'm gone. It's really easy to clean before a friend comes over, but very different preparing for a stranger who would like to pretend they're entering a sterile environment where no one else has ever slept or pooped. I just don't notice the stains on the kitchen cabinets from the coffee maker percolating, because my eyes grow accustomed to them. Culture impacts attentiveness. Most Americans won't dumpster dive for a used mattress, but gladly pay a hotel $150 a night to sleep on one that's seen a lot more action. Bringing it back to seeing my performance through another CRNA's eyes, maybe my mess of syringes or lazy charting doesn't register when someone comes to relieve me, because it's been adequate for my purposes. This sounds silly, but when I'm in a long surgery, I will walk to the door and turn around like I'm entering the room for the first time. Sometimes I pick up on subtle changes in patient condition that way, and it always keeps me better organized. Malcolm Gladwell's *Blink* summarizes research that as we learn to become experts, the brain picks up information at first glance that it can't receive in any other way. Observations of someone else's house or clinical habits are all about perception, which is a main topic in the relationship section but will impact your occupational success.

A common question I've been asked is if it helps to be a nurse at a facility before becoming an anesthesia student. This also relates to self-perception and the perspectives of others. Can you step out of the shadow of your old job? It'll certainly help relationships with the circulators and other nurses, but an incompetent student still will have major problems six months into the program, even if everyone loves her. That's why I spent the last few chapters talking about all the preparations needed before starting school. How you did in nursing clinicals may be a good predictor of where you should take your first job as a registered nurse. The quickest way is to find the ICU where the most critical patients within fifty miles are shipped for advanced care and work there for a year. Realize that your interview for anesthesia school will probably take place within a few months of working your first job as a nurse. For a few nurses (usually those excelling clinically rather than scholastically), this quick transition is best because they're still in "academic mode" from undergraduate education when they start anesthesia school. If you look up statistics from any year from NBCRNA for board pass rates, you'll quickly realize that a long break before going back to school makes passing much more difficult. Of course, still looking like a teenager might make it more difficult for people to take you seriously, so again, there is no substitute for competence. Let's talk about how to develop that.

CRNAs don't really give up on things they need, like control of the airway or a labile blood pressure. It must be something we learned as nurses, pestering a stubborn physician until he or she broke and came to see the patient we had a "hunch" wasn't doing well. Thankfully, the accelerated education I received in anesthesia school has replaced most hunches and notions into evidenced based differential diagnoses. A critical key to staying out of trouble is to always obtain the vascular access you need. Have a plan for the access you want and how to get it back if you lose it. For a case on a sick patient or with potential for the type of blood loss you'd otherwise only see in a horror movie, have a central line/arterial line in the room even if the plan is to just set up for a second IV. If you have the time and an exposed arm, it's certainly fine to wait until the surgeon starts before placing more lines. Unfortunately, this is a fairly rare phenomenon unless the patient is prone with arms extended like an anesthetized Superman (which would never work, if you saw the 2006 movie). The surgical prep and drapes make it harder to place warming devices and orogastric tubes, or slide a magnet over a pacemaker once the surgery starts. What I'm saying is that the period of time from the patient arriving in the OR suite until the surgeon cuts the skin and insults the circulator about the dullness of scalpels nowadays is critical. This length of time differs widely depending on the type of surgery, surgeon, and even the culture of the clinical site. You need to quickly move from one task to another, only stopping to treat the wild variations in vital signs that often occur during this time, paying attention to trends. If you're being patient in administrating a medication or some other task during this time, you probably will want to explain that to your preceptor before they ask why you're not running around like a rabid rhesus monkey. Pathetic as it may sound, you'll look more vigilant frantically double checking everything rather than calmly taking a seat and charting once you've secured the airway, taped the eyes, and immobilized the appendages most likely to punch you once the patient wakes up.

Even as a student, you do need to eventually sit still and focus on mundane tasks like charting. This is when the quality of your visual and auditory monitors matters. More seasoned anesthetists refer to "developing your anesthesia ears" as the sixth sense ability to suddenly focus on a subtle monitor blip or vital sign change. This is how they can fill out a crosswords puzzle while providing excellent care. As a student, terrible things could happen while you search for nine across, so stay focused. No sudoku or Fortnite! Your best monitors are those with current, continual data. Baseline changes in pulse oximetry with breathing can reveal dehydration. Suddenly smaller oscillations can detect bleeding and perfusion problems quicker than your blood pressure cuff can cycle. I suppose that I should back up my assertions in this chapter, so see this study for more on interpreting oximeter waveforms. (If your print version won't let you click on hyperlinks, email me here and I'll send you a scholarship and a profuse apology within the hour). Remember that the few second delay in pulse oximetry means that visualizing heart rate changes on your EKG is the quickest method to see any changes. Those few seconds seem like an eternity when your saturation is still decreasing after you secure a difficult airway! In patients with weak hearts, the pulse ox functions as a time machine telling you what a bad job you were doing thirty seconds ago at ensuring the patient had adequate ventilation. Doing a jaw thrust on a patient with a 100% saturation looks less foolish than the same move on someone reading 50%. We really are spoiled though. It wasn't too long ago that saturation was monitored by patient color and blood pressure by a manual cuff. It's still important to maintain those skills, because equipment will fail, especially with surgeons and techs leaning on patients or causing artifact with electronic equipment. You won't have to change scrubs quite so often if you check nail beds and a carotid pulse for adequate perfusion—although you probably should get that stress incontinence checked before you start clinicals. The decision on whether or not to place an arterial line can be as nebulous as assigning ASA status, depending on the anesthetist or anesthesiologist in charge. Similar to pulse oximetry, an arterial waveform can tell you much more than beat to beat blood pressure. For example, I call an arterial line a "vascular BIS", because you now have access to subtle trend changes much quicker than you otherwise would.

Bispectral Index monitoring may be required at your clinical site for every general anesthesia case performed. Alternatively, other hospitals don't use them at all. As with any device, BIS values need to be compared with all other available monitor data. Bair huggers and IV pumps can cause artifact interpreted as higher than normal values. The point of BIS monitoring is to use less anesthetic agent, not more! Also, even when set to its swiftest setting, the BIS often tells you that a patient is getting light only after they've started doing calisthenics with trocars in their tummy. The monitor is still useful without patient paralysis, but I don't recommend aiming for a value of fifty-five like I'm willing to do with a pleasantly paralyzed patient. An off-label use for the BIS is quickly diagnosing brain death before an impatient or greedy surgeon gets paid to cut on a corpse. Of course, that only works if the patient isn't overly sedated: I've superstitiously used sodium thiopental to bring a BIS to zero right before the surgeon clamped a major artery.

Staying ahead academically will help clear up some of the confusion between anesthetist preference and evidence-based practice. I personally love using Benadryl in most cases and refer to it as "cheap Precedex" because of its many beneficial side effects. That doesn't mean I have a bias against infusions. In fact, dose-response curves result in more even vital signs and consistent results regardless of the drug titrated. Consider carotid surgery, where the more aggressive approach is to alternatively give IV push neosynephrine or nitroglycerin. Although research shows that hypertension can be more harmful than hypotension, whipsawing between the two will definitely lose you style points. Now in my ninth year as a nurse anesthetist, I've noticed that a gradual induction with exactly the doses the patient needs and therefore no need for pressors or beta blockers during the first half hour of the case often means I never need them at all. School will teach you which drugs are appropriate for certain situations, but experience teaches that the dose of drug and when you give it matters even more. One of the bonus items at the back of the book is meant for ICU nurses and talks about our most important medicine: patience or a "tincture of time." I can sedate many extremely sick patients with just propofol if I correctly balance it with the stimulation from a scope going up or down their GI tract.

Despite the expense, an infusion of Precedex, remifentanil, or even propofol and ketamine can blunt wide changes in sympathetic response. Larger doses of Sufenta or even fentanyl exhibit a sympathetic blunting and crisp wake up similar to low-dose anesthetic agent with a remifentanil infusion, but hypotension or narcotization can't be turned off quickly without an infusion. That's why you're paying $34 more for the remifentantil. There are ways to easily use bolus doses of drugs meant for infusions and vice versa, but it does take careful, cautious attention to the individual patient and a personality like mine, as opposed to the "let's get a stable routine down and do it every time" type of clinician. Just like my research article in the finance section, in this new edition I took exclusive research off the publisher's website since they didn't pay me. Now you can enjoy reading about novel, multi-modal approaches to treating pain. Some of you would likely prefer a penile block of Phenergan to reading another academic paper, so rather than paste it here, I uploaded it to archive.org/details/PostOpPain. I've linked it several times, but from that web page you can also find the audio version of this book.

Pharmacoeconomics is crucial in anesthesia because so many techniques work equally well but differ widely in price. A simple illustration is using beta blockers to tame a sudden sympathetic response. Esmolol costs more than longer-acting metoprolol, and the effect wears off much faster (unless you give too much and experience a few moments of sheer terror). Labetelol is not a good substitute because of the residual hypotention. It's short sighted to aim for results that will dissipate with the sevoflurane vapor at the end of the case. Because of this, I tend to give more narcotics than most because pain control is useful in recovery. Amnesia isn't, unless you did a horrible job and don't want the patient remembering anything. That approach fell out of favor in the 1930's, when scopolamine infusions were commonly administered to laboring patients scorning traditional midwives in favor of fancy hospital births.

The same rationale of a pain and drama free recovery exists for a multi-modal technique in institutions with quick patient turnover, if the pharmacy department doesn't keep the anesthesia department's perineal organs in her purse. In the long run, it doesn't matter if the patient, the hospital, or the insurance company benefits from equal care at a lower price—the end result is keeping health care costs down and knowing how to use a broader arsenal of drugs when inevitable shortages occur. Even if an approach of oral Neurontin and Benadryl coupled with IV acetaminophen and Precedex costs more, the quicker discharge and lower incidence of pain, opioid addiction, and nausea may still save money. Don't worry much about costs as a student though. Besides, your experience as a nurse should supply you with all sorts of non-pharmacological ways to increase quality of care, especially during sedation cases. A Bair hugger keeping the patient cozy can do wonders, and that gentle roaring sound masks many an "Oops" or "$%*&$!" from the surgeon. Especially during propofol shortages, I've learned that comfortable and tired patients need a smaller amount of our more powerful drugs. Inducing drowsiness with Phenergan or droperidol can make your care more complex, however, so sometimes my boring small talk saves the day.

People have strong opinions about niche drugs, but every drug will burn you sooner or later because each patient is different. Before I try to clumsily segue from the topic of drugs to that of emergence, I have advice for one last class of drugs: antiemetics. Most of these drugs make patients sleepy, which is cheating because then they're snoring too loud to complain about nausea, pain, or an acute need for frozen treats. The best method seems to be combining several agents with a low dose propofol infusion: higher than 50 micrograms/kg/min for more than 400mg worth can occasionally cause a delayed emergence (as easily evidenced by the patient's failure to breathe at the end of the case). If the corresponding decrease in anesthetic gas makes you nervous, use a BIS to give as little agent as possible. I use this technique along with narcotics stereotypically in some patients. For every awkward tattoo or piercing, I titrate their own respiratory rate a breath lower, aiming for a value between eight and twelve by extubation. If giving less narcotic, multi-modal approaches make titration by respiratory rate less useful. It's worth the trade-off, and opioid-free anesthetics continue to decrease adverse outcomes. Recent data in military personnel with combat experience suggests ketamine for this purpose, but that's a dumb idea until you've gained more experience. Because the AANA article I'm referring to is at least ten feet away from me right now, you'll have to amuse yourself with the citations at the end of this chapter instead.

Most textbooks recommend keeping a patient's own respiratory rate at twelve, so take my bias against crazy patients with a grain of salt or similar powder. Wide ranges of preferences come to play when emerging a patient from anesthesia. Don't get rattled when one anesthetist tells you to keep the gas on for a few more minutes and the next asks you why you didn't turn the vaporizer off five minutes ago (my personal preference). Waking up the patient on time is easier with drugs that don't vary in their effect depending on liver enzymes, the way that benzodiazepines do. Whether you learn to get a patient breathing spontaneously at the end of a case or blow the gas off with the ventilator, the object is to avoid a rook versus queen situation. My chess skills peaked in the fifth grade, mostly because better players put me in situations where I had to let one of my better pieces die to save another. In anesthesia, you never want to be left with several poor options as your only alternatives. Should I keep the tube in as the patient clumsily emerges and their heart rate resembles a hummingbird, or do I take it out and hope everything gets better? Look at airway algorithms or even the last few choices in ACLS and you'll understand. Minor problems should be immediately addressed before you end up poking holes in your patient's neck so they'll breathe or scouring the pharmacy for bretylium.

So what is your goal? Again, analogies best explain how to keep your patient out of trouble. Have you ever held your breath underwater? If you just lie there, floating limply until your friends worriedly shake you (or snicker, depending on your quality of friends), you might last a few minutes without air. On the other hand, try frantically paddling beneath the surface and it won't be long until you feel the urge to breathe in crisp blue pool water. A patient coughing during emergence quickly burns up oxygen reserves, not just style points. You'll notice a similar phenomenon as your patients wiggle during a rapid sequence induction. This is also true in MAC cases, where a large patient flailing around instead of quietly accepting a bronchoscope can desaturate quicker than you can soil your scrubs.

Whether putting a tube in or taking it out, don't ever risk a problem you can't fix. In both intubating and masking a patient, the third identical attempt has similar results to the first, so you need to change your angle (and your blade, whether a full screen view with a Miller or a wide screen with a Mac), like a brick wall effortlessly floating down a river. Had enough analogies? Just remember, masking unsuccessfully is like trying to break through that brick wall with your head. That didn't make sense to me either. You'll just have to experience it.

Citation Sources:

http://tinyurl.com/wackypulseox1
http://tinyurl.com/ASAbisuses
http://www.usaisr.amedd.army.mil/battle_pain_management.html
http://youtu.be/5cFGGOEvVyI

Excelling as a Student

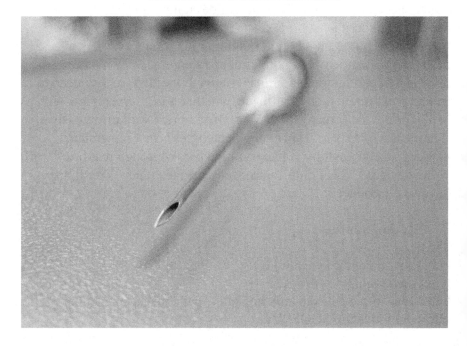

"Be wise as serpents and innocent as doves." Those words of Jesus are a good motto. Have you ever been woken up by the loud sound of a serpent chirping at day break? Ever heard of anyone killed by a dove? I mentioned earlier that the admissions interview, at least in a postbaccalaureate program, is usually more important than your GPA and GRE/MCAT etc. In part, it's because programs don't want difficult students who use up valuable time that should be split equally among all the students. That said, most program directors estimate 80% of their time goes to 20% of their students. You can teach anyone technical skills like stitching or placing invasive lines. Connecting the clinical dots like an episode of *House* (hopefully with fewer pain meds and wisecracks) or improving a surly attitude is considerably harder. That doesn't mean you're a shoo-in to graduate if you're happy and attractive, but a charming personality goes a long way. A friend of mine became irritated at the difficult (and irrelevant) clinical questions she was asked during her anesthesia interview—needless to say, she's still working as an ICU nurse. Being a successful student involves being polite to people you'd rather stomp on every day. Should you mask your personality the way you would an unruly pediatric patient? My clinical director always quoted a famous phrase from one of John Wayne's movies. "Speak low, speak slow, and don't say too much." Fly under the radar as much as possible.

"Over time, you'd begin to notice and pay attention to body language and demeanors. You'd start to focus on faces—not just to read lips, but to look at people's eyes and *in* their eyes. When you become so dependent on interpreting a person's face in order to truly converse, you really begin to pick up on how people look when they are angry, sad, happy, or even lying." —Sarah Churman in *Powered On.*

Although Sarah is talking about learning to communicate despite profound hearing loss, the concept holds true for navigating the foreign world of health care. This can be especially trying when everyone is wearing surgical masks and garb that make discerning non-verbal cues even more difficult. What did that uplifted eyebrow mean? It's almost like reverting to a self-conscious teenager trying to decide whether to be bold and assertive or quiet and studious.

Sorry for the memories of Clearasil, but exactly what traits and attitudes increase the chances for success? It's easier to blend in if you look like you belong. Dyeing your hair gray or styling it into a matronly bun to look older is a bit much, but adopt the mannerisms and vernacular of your preceptors and professors. Don't overdo it or you'll lose the politeness you need as a student—an employee describing an unhealthy patient as "a manatee, only grayer" doesn't give you the license to categorize patients by their resemblance to varied marine life. Although, I am partial to playful sea otters. See where the line is? You let your technical vocabulary be influenced by the university or hospital, but not your attitude. You won't always feel cheerful and enthusiastic as you train for free beside highly paid yet grumpy and jaded professionals. Judgments about your work ethic will start with your first handshake, so there's no time to gradually exhibit an eagerness to work and learn.

41

I've always looked at the task of remaining upbeat and gracious in the face of injustice and adversity as a spiritual one. James 1:2 says to count it as joy when we face trials. Use the hardship of school to make you a better and happier person regardless of your present circumstance. Whatever your beliefs may be, you need a strong sense of ethics to deliver compassionate patient care while learning complex information and having your skills constantly scrutinized.

Staying true to yourself is still possible even while exuding a hard-working, people-loving student persona. I want to stress that it's not a façade, but rather a persistence of behavior that may not reflect your true feelings moment by moment. The habit of being resourceful and energized in the classroom and at clinicals makes life easier and allows you more freedom to express your individuality. I play the role of a reserved professional when needed these days, but I'm quite accomplished in the art of being silly as well. Take into consideration this excerpt from my first book, *Nonsense*:

"Before Ice from Heaven breathed life into the snowmen and death to the villagers, one of the craftsmen brought his young human child to the Field of Sculpture. The result was Klite, small yet round of form and incontinent of bowel. The other snow children all had legs and were warned to run away from the pretty brown icicles that resulted, but despite many medicines and reconstructive surgeries, Klite's problem continued."

Come on! How ridiculous is that? Channeled correctly, my weirdness made for creative presentations and papers in graduate school. For my nursing degree, however, I often took it too far. I vaguely recall stating a research hypothesis with a rap video featuring snowmen displaying gang symbols. In my defense, we were studying urban youth in cold weather, and my professor was whiter than artificial snow at a ski resort. In graduate school, the last few paragraphs I've written about appropriate behavior are just as important in the classroom as the clinical site. More learning comes from research studies and is the responsibility of the student at this level. Grades depend on professor's opinions of papers and presentations, not just objective test scores.

I probably don't need to discuss the importance of studying, since you won't last very long in any program if you're stupid. Keep in mind though that it's not the smartest, but the most committed, hard-working, and relentless students who do best in school. That sentence is probably more valuable than everything else in this book. I didn't naturally have those tendencies, but I still have a few of those stubborn characteristics today because of the habits I had to develop as a student. If you're a competitive individual, think of it as part of the challenge, like a game. Especially for important tests, framing them as a chance to show your expertise rather than potential for abysmal failure will calm your nerves and make you easier to live with. In a grueling program, you may be spending more time with your classmates than your loved ones. Having a reputation of not playing well with others is hard to shake. Should you force yourself to join study groups even if you don't learn well that way? Not unless there's free food involved. However, as much as it depends on you, try to keep the relationship with your classmates as healthy and encouraging as you can. Without a degree of friendship and trust, you'll miss out on all of the knowledge you can share with each other. You know, the important things like which professor to avoid and what the idiosyncrasies/paranoid delusions of a certain clinical preceptor are.

Ugh. Writing about all the things you should do is wearing me out! How do you pace yourself to prevent a breakdown from all the smiling and studying and simpering? Well, you don't at first. Worry about pacing yourself once you get feedback in the form of grades and skill evaluations. Hearing nothing is good, but critique yourself, even socially, while pursuing a wide array of experiences to fill the gaping knowledge holes you don't even know about yet. I distinctly remember blowing out candles and philosophizing on my fifth birthday that I was pretty much as smart as I was going to get.

Similar to a job interview, know your weaknesses but guard them; don't give preceptors ammunition to use against you. Rather than carving out time for such navel gazing in the heat of battle, take some personality tests before you start school, if possible. Real ones, not the type revealing which dystopian heroine you most resemble. We'll discuss the relative merits of understanding yourself with the help of a counselor later, but free, validated tests include an adapted Myers-Brigg Test on 16personalities.com, Enneagrams on 9types.com, and graphs of personality factors on personalityfactors.com. You don't want to be deficient clinically because of a weak area, so it's a balance between acknowledging and strengthening areas that need improvement. Because I'm not obsessive-compulsive or have a Type-A personality, I encourage students to try new techniques or medicines when we work together, provided they're safe and acceptable options for the patient, of course. However, my personality also means that I'm easily ignored until I prove my expertise and can quietly direct a room to save a patient.

Several personality types share the flaw of assuming others share their perspective. I can't read minds, and I don't always know my own perspective, much less grasp the nuances of how I am perceived. Think critically and change priorities as new information presents itself by understanding your unique patterns. For most nurses, doing an excellent job serves as adequate inspiration to continue excellence, but sustained sustained competence bores me. Rather than maintaining the status quo and following rules I might not care for, my philosophy leans toward, "If it's not broke—let's break it and fix it and it'll be so much better." Knowing that my strength of creative, individualized care and problem solving comes with the weakness of brinksmanship and possible instability, I can "train my brain" to remain objective when I need to make a clinical decision or finish one task rather than incompletely try for an IV, call for help, and start drawing up a medicine simultaneously.

Academically you need to excel or none of this matters. This is more important before you get accepted into your terminal degree program. If you have a 3.0 GPA, unless every other aspect of your resume, experience, interview, and knowledge is impeccable, you won't be accepted into a competitive program (not that you shouldn't try). It's difficult for employers to really compare GPAs from various master's level programs though. A hospital based program will have a local school provide the classes, but those classes might be an afterthought depending on a schedule that will allow the students to work for free, er, learn clinically as much as possible. Another program with more control over clinical sites might make sure not to overload students before important tests so they can concentrate on learning didactic and clinical information. This differs among specialties: nursing students tend to be rarely useful and control by clinical sites is minimal, while at the other extreme we all know how medical residents are treated.

Setting aside time to study takes discipline. I've been known to take study materials to weddings and funerals. It's not like you can invite friends over and practice intubating or catheterizing different orifices to improve your clinical skills. If you do see such an opportunity on Craigslist, I suggest you pass on it. It can be especially difficult when studying for boards or other standardized tests. I took my GRE as a nineteen year old sophomore because of the financial incentives for achieving my terminal degree quickly. Also, I wasn't going to be learning any new math skills in the future. I did very well, which forced my hand to get into graduate school quickly since, for many schools, GRE scores expire in five years. Doing poorly isn't the death of your dreams—schools realize that people exhibit their brilliance in different ways. The day before my first final exam in nursing school, I sat in the library all day and read my textbook cover to cover. Other people learn better with flashcards or by discussing topics in study groups. Your learning style may favor theoretical knowledge or a particular skill set. Most healthcare careers in a hospital feature a combination of the two. As an illustration, a nurse practitioner hired by a hospital may find herself placing invasive lines in an ICU or acting as a first assistant in the OR, but in an office setting, physical skills may be limited to a thorough physical assessment and require less kinesthetic learning. So, if you were kicked off the cheerleading team because you couldn't remember the correct sequence of back flips and round outs, advanced nerve block techniques and pain management might not be the right specialty for you. However, if you're in a program (like nurse anesthesia) that requires mastery of many specialties without the choice of electives, the goal should not be to avoid areas you suspect may be difficult for you. If complex concepts like critical care medicine are a problem area, you'll simply have to work harder at it than your classmates might. This is where forming good relationships with your classmates comes in. It's true that you may be able to explain pathophysiology better than a clinical skill, but the act of teaching will hone your skills.

It helps to have goals to keep yourself accountable. If you like writing and journaling, make this into a more formal process, in the rare case that you're willing to write or read anything not related to school. Journaling is also a way to check in with yourself and prevent the hideous transformation from ignorant but nice to minimally competent and mean that occurs in some residencies. A short term goal might be to increase your rapport with patients for the week. Long term goals are more useful to self evaluate your progress. I know several advanced practice nurses who returned to regular nursing jobs because they felt they were unqualified once they graduated. Don't be confused, I know I said earlier that the academic standards are fairly similar between schools. (Honestly, especially with online learning, this is much less true in 2018 than in 2012). You still have to work as hard as you can to emerge from school as competent as possible. Part of the problem with my colleagues was their salaries. They worked so many hours for their physician bosses that they realized an hourly wage as a nurse made more money, once overtime was considered. You won't have these problems because of the previous chapters on wisely choosing health careers and managing tuition costs carefully, but every facility is different.

Switching clinical sites can be nerve wracking, especially if you don't like change. It's helpful as a clinician because different facilities have varying ways of doing things and different areas of expertise. That way you can pick and choose the methods that work best. The disadvantage is the time it takes to decipher new monitors, charting, and procedures. The clientele can differ drastically too, even if the unit is identical. Case in point, I worked as an agency nurse in two large Surgical Intensive Care Units within ten miles of each other. The patients in the first SICU were mostly elderly patients with chronic diseases recovering from routine surgeries. In the second, many of the patients were healthier but acutely recovering from major surgeries. The drugs and therapies implemented on these two groups rarely overlapped. If you have the opportunity to pick rotations, aim for contrasts, as large trauma hospitals, academic specialty centers, and small offices all have individual nuances that will make you a better practitioner.

If you have a choice between clinical sites that both have a culture of belittling students, the better choice may be the larger facility. The novelty of fresh meat to bully will fade quicker. There are limited resources on what your options are in bullying situations, which is why I've created some with some highly trained colleagues. See the "About the Author" section for more information. The social structure of the OR places students right below the good people who mop the floors between cases, and there is little improvement as you move to other areas of the hospital.

I was asking an anesthesia student about this the other day, mostly because I was running out of ideas for this part of the book. She explained quite eloquently the best option for a student to practice on the professors and preceptors who target them: absence seizures. Sometimes you just need a moment to collect your thoughts before blurting out the wrong answer to a difficult question. Watch some political debates and you'll master your stalling skills quickly. Alternatively, I suppose you could study more. Learning with your fellow students will improve that tricky skill of opening your mouth and having the correct knowledge from your brain flow out.

All that knowledge provides wonderful benefits, the least of which is invitations to join honor societies. I'll talk more about resumes and curriculum vitas in the "First Job" chapter, but if you're typing in size eight font, you're doing it wrong. It's a much better idea to join a prestigious society that you barely qualify for rather than shelling out money so you can add "The Golden Key Honor Society" (which only requires an embarrassing 3.0 GPA for membership) to your list of accomplishments. Pay attention or you'll end up pawning all those honor cords for Ramen. My first year of college, I joined the Alpha Lambda Delta Honor Society. It made me look better as I applied for scholarships and I still have it on my CV today, so it was worth my $75 or whatever it cost back then. As a junior, I was eligible for the nursing honor society! There was going to be a ceremony and all of my eligible classmates were really excited about the opportunity. I knew I was destined for graduate school so I reasoned I'd be more willing to part with hard-earned money next time around. Several years later, the opportunity did repeat itself, but I realized I hadn't missed anything by not being a member and had little to gain from becoming one.

Please understand that my cheap and practical nature only makes sense from a clinical standpoint. Honor societies and similar organizations hold a wealth of opportunities if pursuing an academic or managerial position in health care. As an undergraduate, I was very active on campus and even started a speech and debate team with my brother. If meetings and networking with smart people is your thing, then invest not only your money but your time as well with an organization. You probably won't have any activities in graduate school, but even at the collegiate level, don't waste your time on organizations that fit in that nebulous area between "resume padder" and "beneficial group that I enjoy".

I've talked about being efficient in your studying and your organizations. Unless you have a leadership position—ooh, I just remembered that I was vice president of communication for my nursing class. Apparently, I didn't do anything important or get very far with that impressive title since I forgot all about it until now. I wonder if it's too late to get my money back. Speaking of money, be wary of all the board preparation programs and classes you can buy. For about $100, I bought Prodigy: three online tests that simulated anesthesia boards. I researched every answer choice and studied much harder than I otherwise would have, since I didn't go to the expensive conferences most of my classmates attended to help them pass the NCE. I simply don't learn by hearing people lecture, although that format was a splendid cure for my sleep deprivation.

So, if you go to a board review conference, don't party all night long before or during. I only know of one colleague who learned better when slightly drunk, and the dose he needed increased with time. Alcohol is cheaper than an Adderall prescription, but remember that one of your goals from the first chapter is to avoid being a broken mess by the time you graduate. I had study materials with me at all times, but mixing social and study times rarely worked. Neither did mixing work and study times, but at least I got paid during a sleepy night shift as I read *Miller's Anesthesia*.

Lastly, efficiency extends to your grades and relationships. How are they related? Every semester, I would barely squeak by with the grade I wanted to obtain. If some of my classmates received a 100% on a test and I received a 93.5000001%, I would inform them that I was smarter because they studied too much to get the same grade I received. That same philosophy is the key to winning games like *Settlers of Catan*. While your neighbors are on a romantic getaway in Aruba, you may be splurging by shelving the textbooks and playing board games for a night. You're not going to receive an A+ in relationships with friends and family during school. Just do whatever it takes so you don't graduate lonely. Thankfully, I was an exception because I was used to a long distance relationship, so the limited time I had for a local relationship during school was actually an improvement.

Picking up the Charred Remains after You Crash and Burn

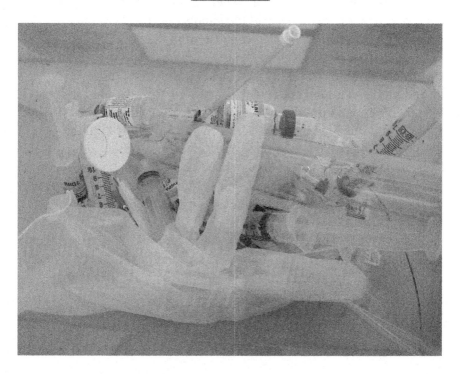

Angry red pen filled the piece of paper I held in my shaking hands! Clinical evaluations had finally arrived. I'd been doing much better, but it was always difficult for me to tell if my preceptors agreed. As I read the criticisms, a cold chill seeped through me. It was over. I could fight this for the next eighteen months, but my eventual dismissal was a stark possibility if this was what the anesthetists thought of me. Better to leave now and cut my losses.

Thankfully it would only take a few months to make up the financial losses from school. Rather than taking time off to mourn the death of a dream, I started working as an agency nurse the day after I finished my semester and turned in my letter of resignation. Obviously that's one advantage of pursuing a higher degree in nursing as opposed to PA or medical school. I reasoned that if I could adjust clinically from the operating room to a nursing floor as a reviled but highly-paid substitute, I would still consider a career requiring clinical expertise. Being assigned to multiple areas in a hospital without knowing any of the policies and procedures stretched my skills farther than working in a world class cardiac surgery unit ever did.

But how did this happen and where did I go wrong? I aced my classes with a 4.0, certainly had the support of my classmates, and I was rarely stumped by a difficult question in class or clinicals. My skills at IV placement, endotracheal intubations, and other necessary abilities were on par with my classmates. However, the skills I lacked included all the etiquette and ways to deflect attention I've already mentioned in this book. I was the youngest and silliest student, and received the most scrutiny in the quest to find the weakest links unable to shoulder the great responsibility of a nurse anesthetist. We all knew that our particular program had a custom of losing a few students every year, not unlike sacrificing a slave or two to ensure a bountiful harvest. This isn't rare of course, especially with advanced and specialized degrees. I'd like to say that I was unfairly judged as only being "book smart", but it's true that clinical expertise is much more vital in anesthesia than in similar occupations. I sometimes struggled in putting the whole clinical picture together and at hiding that struggle, since any admission of weakness would place me one step closer to that sacrificial alter. Despite my calm exterior, I started getting rattled by preceptors who would demand perfection in the way I secured tubes or worded my charting.

"The whole picture" can be interpreted to mean all sorts of crucial or irrelevant details. You can understand research and theory and skillfully ascultate heart sounds, compound medicines, adjust spines, or perform other job-specific tasks without being a competent practitioner. Consider the dangerous backlog of patients waiting to be seen in a busy ER if a PA isn't quick enough to examine them all in time. Of course, there isn't a manual on how to prioritize or be efficient without sacrificing meticulousness. Working in healthcare consists of stringing a list of tasks together in the safest and most expedient way possible. Sometimes shortcuts must be ignored to do jobs right. The trouble starts when you fall behind and your prioritization degrades from taking care of the most critical issues first to behavior that most closely resembles "Whack-A-Mole". On a side note, I've always earned many more tickets on that game by using both hands and recruiting a friend than swinging that stupid foam mallet all day.

One solution to keep that task string from infarcting is to set up for success at the beginning of the day. This involves getting to class or clinicals earlier than necessary so you can troubleshoot any particular problems. Honestly, with all I've learned and experienced, I still don't do this, but maybe eventually I'll become one of those conscientious people who arrive at work a half hour early to sip coffee, read the newspaper, and ease into their day. I get more exercise than them by consistently sprinting to the time clock every morning. Anyway, by arriving early you can double check equipment, find that elusive drug or monitor that you need, and set up for the first patient you'll see.

Another way to avoid crashing and burning is to memorize a general sequence of tasks and events. Write it down too. This helped me as a new nurse trying to receive report, check labs, assess my patients, and pass out their morning medicines all by 10:00. If I thought through several possibilities to efficiently plan my day, it was easier to deal with detours without have to repeat steps. So, if it was a busy day and a patient cheerfully pooped themselves at 7:45, they would be awarded with a bath, routine medicine and a physical assessment, pain medication if they needed it, and of course clean sheets. We had a one hour window to pass out 9:00 am meds and you'll notice that my plan just violated it. Before you cast me into the dreaded nurse float pool, understand that the alternative would be to wait fifteen minutes and probably give the other patients their medicines thirty minutes late due to inefficiency. These "shortcuts" also worked in the ER, another department were I had to occasionally choose one noble task over another that I knew I'd never get around to completing. The patient in bed space five is probably still waiting on his orange juice.

After such sacrilegious subject matter, you may wonder why I advocate spending so much time learning the best way to do things if great plans often degenerate into a free for all. It's important to learn good habits while you have a preceptor making sure you follow them. This limits the eventual shortcuts you might be tempted to take in the name of expediency. You probably thought I was going to again force the word "efficiency" into that last sentence. Same difference, but as I mentioned in the first few pages, the point of this book is not to be a guide for how to barely graduate! Rather, work to become an expert in the classroom and clinical setting.

So what would have saved me? A fairer system might have. One preceptor told me I should become a waiter to increase my time management skills. I needed more life experiences, really, and that included some failure. Not to sound arrogant, but I'd never really failed before. In high school, I entered a speech meet and had major deductions because I didn't know any of the rules and had never tried it before. I still won the event and had similar success in college in anything I put my mind to.

You're probably an overachiever if you're reading this book (or a nosy coworker of mine). Previously for me, failure academically was losing my 4.0 in college because OB nursing was so boring. I've met many people who chose health care as a second or third career option. Word it however you'd like, there has to be some failure involved to no longer use a law or accounting degree. In one case, she was a stripper first, so the decision to stabilize vital signs rather than disturb them was a move in the right direction. In today's workplace, most people change careers at least once in their lifetime. Although I tried to console myself with these facts, I still felt humiliated that I tried something and failed. I didn't intend to make this part of the book so deeply personal, but objective writing on this subject doesn't really help as much as support from someone who has been there. So many nurses have shared how inspirational my multiple screw ups have been.

With the exception of eccentric artists and musicians, I have no patience for those who sulk and go off to find themselves after a setback. You can have time off when you retire or die—until then, you need to make money so you can eat and gain experience. Within two weeks, I was back at that same toxic clinical site, this time as an agency nurse instead of an anesthesia student. It was difficult to absorb the pitying stares and swirling rumors. "Why did he quit? Was it an affair, did he kill a patient, was it because his warm Greek tan turns a strange shade of green under OR lights?"

Maybe no one asked that last question, but I found solace in noting that it was much more awkward for my former preceptors than it was for me. My classmates told me I was sorely missed—close knit relationships were a plus at my school, even if the cause was similar to hostages bonding together. I found myself cagily answering questions the way smart nurses answer, "So, are you applying for anesthesia school?" It's dumb to lie, because if you're accepted they'll figure it out. At the same time, nosy people don't really deserve a long answer that objectively answers their questions. Multiple people looked at my situation and told me I'd be certain to win if I sued. I wasn't sure what I'd win—this wasn't Whack-A-Mole, and besides, 2,000 tickets is barely enough to win a whoopee cushion! I just lost some of you who haven't visited "Chuck E. Cheese" within the last few years, er, as a child.

Either way, it's important to fix what depends on you rather than blaming others. You can't sue your way to your goal. Now that I do a lot of corporate wellness work, I have come to admire the value of a sternly worded legal letter, but revenge as a motivator corrupts the soul. I've known people who decided to stick it out in clinical programs that obviously were not a good fit. It was ugly, embarrassing, expensive, and difficult to explain on transcripts and resumes. I left my first foray into graduate school on my own terms for my own reasons long before it came to that. And yes, it's true that I might have lasted until graduation from anesthesia school. I simply realized that I had no desire to hang on by the skin of my teeth when Plan B, C, and D could all easily provide for my financial needs. Because of that, I came through that experience with no regrets. Put down the syringe of Haldol and let me explain! I needed life experience and more varied clinical experiences. My didactic knowledge was impeccable and my clinical skills marginal. No matter how great a career in anesthesia seemed, was it really worth going from an all-star to a benchwarmer until my mediocrity possibly hurt a patient?

With that in mind, I purposely took the toughest traveling assignments in my part of the state. Compared to the rigors of anesthesia school, it felt like playing T-ball instead of Major League Baseball. I took online classes to continue my master's degree, but I hadn't decided what I should specialize in. I could easily finish a nurse clinician degree in a year, because research had always been one of my strengths. Because of my grades and experience in public speaking, the graduate program wanted me to stay, get a PhD, and become a professor. I'd always liked teaching, but it takes a special person to learn that much nursing theory. Like any young person would do in a 1960's sitcom, I decided to ask my neighbor for advice.

Ok, so it wasn't as random as I'm making it out to be. She was about to graduate from another anesthesia school, and I'd worked with her husband, who was also a nurse. She listened to my story and said,

"I wish I could have talked you into going with me to my school instead. It's not the nightmare for students that yours is, so if you're willing to try again we interview next year's class in a few months."

I wish I could tell you that from then on I lived happily ever after, but I can't. I talked to my girlfriend about it, because this would further alter the glorious timeline in my head about marrying once I finished graduate school. Did I want to become a CRNA this bad? I'd never talked to a single person who overestimated how grueling and consuming school was—did I really want to do it twice? But I did, I really did, so once again I was interviewing flawlessly, but this time I didn't care. Nothing mattered until clinicals started.

"How would you describe the anesthetists at your previous clinical site?" one skeptical interviewer asked.

"Capricious", I responded. My acceptance letter arrived in the mail a few days later.

Relax, I'm not going to continue a blow by blow account of the epochs I spent as an anesthesia student, although I was giddier the second time in anesthesia school (and more awesome). I graduated with honors, even though my gangster snowman reappeared in a few clinical presentations. You should always have a sense of humor, but it shouldn't come as a surprise to anyone that I overdo it. It takes very little to make me guffaw or giggle like a school girl, so when a vial of Versed came up missing at one of my new clinical sites, guess who the prime suspect was? It didn't help that I ran into some of the same anesthetists I'd worked with during my first attempt at anesthesia school years earlier—thank God I hadn't torched those bridges like I wanted to for their preferential treatment of other students over me! Resentment and bitterness will cloud your concentration and clinical judgment and poison your soul. They do make for some great lyrics though, hence my aforementioned excusal of despondent musicians. Great sayings too, similar to, "It's ok to burn just a few bridges—it keeps the crazies from following you".

I realize that most people won't have a second chance at the same vocation like I did, so I want to talk for a minute about changing careers and making the most of it. I never stopped taking classes or even stopped working other than the very beginning and very end of my scholastic adventures. What can I say, I'm allergic to loans: they make me rashy. We've already talked about piling on more debt and education as a solution for a job that's boring or not working out. Another common response to an unfulfilling career is to go at it alone. Nursing in particular has no entrepreneurial training, while chiropractors and dentists are more accustomed to starting their own businesses. Massage therapists and similar certifications have fairly limited income potential unless they launch their own businesses.

For an example from my specialty, starting a small anesthesia practice with a few buddies is a great plan. You just need a gastroenterologist or optomologist, knowledge of your state's nurse practice laws, and you're all set. The problems start when insurance companies delay your payments for six months because they need to reach an arbitrary 20% claims denied quota. If you have a spouse making a steady income, there's more flexibility to earn profits and make mistakes on your own. Needless to say, I don't recommend this approach if you're still in debt.

It may be enough to have the perspective of an outsider. One of my good friends is an agency pharmacist, traveling to whichever drug store has a shortage for the day. If he doesn't like a particular store, he doesn't go back. The best part of contract work is going to work purposefully, because it's your choice, as opposed to dragging yourself to work because the schedule demands it. I admit, the difference is mostly psychological. I more often worked without contracts. Occasionally, this meant I worked more shifts than were good for my health if I was unsure when the next opportunity would come my way. Working at a higher rate of pay but with a sporadic schedule is only an advantage when there is something valuable to do with time better spent working. For me it was studying, for you it might be seeing those kids you made before starting school.

The last topic in this chapter is probably unnecessary to many of you picking up the charred remains of a futile career. However, it's a question I'm asked frequently because of my experience with holistic health businesses. Is it lucrative to start playing for the other team? Many physician practices have abandoned the insurance model for complementary medicine cash practices centered around supplements and nutraceuticals. Speaking from experience, alternative health companies are just as difficult as starting any other business, but remember the short section about religious beliefs? It's just as important here, so grab your crystals and herbs and prepare for transport! Ok, it's not really that bad, but there's a long continuum between fraudulent and fantastic. If this is a topic of interest, useful alternative medicine clinical skills should be a priority if you have a health degree. A nursing license has more credibility than a string of letters following your name that probably stand for "I Picked up a Degree in Holistic Feta Cheese Management at the International Deli." By "useful alternative medicine skills", I'm referring to one of the several established organizations that promote patient wellness through their proprietary supplements, muscle testing, or allergy-finding techniques. Even a late night infomercial on colon cleanses or diet shakes has a few adherents, so research on your part is needed. If you did not complete a healthcare degree before turning to alternative medicine, a relevant degree or easily understood certificate in something normal should be the priority. If you choose an unaccredited school, be up front about it to your clients.

Whatever you do, don't abandon college credits like a box full of kittens. They expire; useless degrees don't, even if you drop everything to run a hypnosis studio in your parent's garage. Insurance rates differ widely depending on the potential consequences of your business. If you have a small practice doing something boring, they won't be interested in you. If you're an acupuncturist or a budding herbalist taking the types of patients Western medicine can't do anything more with, you need to spend some time assessing your liability. My point? Find your niche, and work tirelessly until you achieve it. Love or greed won't be enough to excel. Facing your fear, which for me was rejection and failure, may prove lucrative as you shape your dream job into what people are willing to pay for.

Your First Job

You did it! Now that you've thrown off your student shackles, you can finally tell everyone what you think of them! Well, maybe not. No matter what glorious title you've obtained, you can't go around telling everyone off. As the newbie, sooner or later you'll need someone, and they may be more inclined to help you if some shreds of humbleness from your residency still remain. No one wants to hear about your wonderful techniques until you get some experience, even if you think you came from the most difficult, cutting edge program in the world. Hospitals often have their own personalities, and your primary job is to continue to collect a paycheck. For example, I finished the last chapter by talking about alternative medicine. I studied textbooks and herbal dictionaries, researched applications for anesthesia and started pilot studies, but I didn't share any of that knowledge until I finished my first year on the job. Nobody needs to be labeled as the group's witch doctor or mad scientist as soon as they start their terminal career (though I'm comfortable with those titles now).

To make life easier, treat everyone as if they are charming and attractive. People may still be mean to you, but they'll look much more awkward if you remain cheerful. Now, the last time I used the word "cheerful" in this book, it was to describe a happily incontinent patient. Don't be flippant, but it's much harder to lecture someone if they're upbeat, even if the odor of their mistake is impossible to overlook. People want to know that you're enthusiastic about your new job and happy to learn. Balance that with assertiveness, because even on your first day, no one should get in the way of the care you deliver to patients. I honestly tell my patients that I will only take care of them if I am confident that I will do a better job than anyone else. If I see a colleague employing a useful technique, I immediately ask them to show me their blend of drugs or angle of catheter insertion (I'm talking about IVs and arterial lines, not foleys, you weirdo). Anyway, that's the strict standard you should hold yourself and others to, while remaining gracious. Lately I've had to practice that more. Otherwise, witty responses and my disarming nature insulate me from hearing useful and necessary criticism.

Healthcare is difficult enough without judgment and rumors being passed around. Any information you receive will be biased. As I neared graduation at my second anesthesia school, many of us discussed how a local anesthesia group had accounting issues for employee benefits. Other than that, it was a great place to work, so a humorous dynamic ensued where we tried to dissuade each other from interviewing there as we all surreptitiously sent the group our curriculum vitae. If that's the first time you've heard that foreign phrase, it's an academically oriented resume once you have an advanced degree. You can finally stop detailing your role as a fast food specialty chef to future employers! Speaking of academics, if you're research driven you may want to consider somewhere where they do that. It's a bit harder to grow as a practitioner at a place chosen by your coworkers because they can relax without having to teach anyone or learn new techniques. Be aware that there are a lot more politics in academic centers, and the chain of command between residents, mid-level practitioners, various students, etc. can be confusing. If you do have residents or students, keep in mind that many preceptors went out of their way to help you learn, and you need to return the favor. Teaching also teaches you, with the exception of a high school chemistry test I bombed while my pretty tutee received 100%.

Your desire to work at a teaching hospital will be heavily influenced by the school you selected. A small school can't offer you the cutting edge research, tools, and surgeries found at a large academic institution. A large school is less likely to expose you to the autonomous experience of a nurse anesthetist in rural America. So, if you've always dreamed of practicing in the heart of New York City, the University of Iowa's program probably wasn't the best fit. Both extremes require unique competence that rarely overlaps. I noticed this gap early on and tried to fill it in my nursing experience by contrasting specific ICU work with floor work at a facility that featured a narcoleptic hospitalist: I'd run the codes until the combination of her vibrating pager, monitor alarms, and the sound of frantic nurses running up the hallway woke her up by the second round of chest compressions. My favorite irony from that particular facility was the imposing religious statue looking over the parking lot who consistently failed to prevent theft and break-ins, but that's another story.

Sorry about the tangent there. I try to obtain both types of experiences at my facility. Our trauma and craniotomy patients require specific expertise with the help of our very involved anesthesiologists. When I tire of teamwork, I find myself enjoying the relative solitude and autonomy afforded in the dreary basement by the hospital's endoscopy center, aka "The Butt Hut". Often, there is less flexibility in older and more established groups. They may feature graduates from a limited number of local institutions and are more conservative and uniform in treatment options, as are specialty centers like pediatric hospitals. Smaller, newly formed groups are more likely to try newer techniques outside of a research setting. Don't interpret this as giving sub-optimal care to sick patients. You need to be flexible with drugs, equipment, and techniques, especially in today's environment of sudden recalls and shortages, but not at a patient's expense. If you need to try something your colleagues haven't seen before, make sure you have the research to back it up. That doesn't mean I take pains to always justify myself now that I'm more experienced—unless someone is honestly curious, I often respond to their criticism by bowing my head, closing my eyes, and whispering reverently, "That's how the Spirit moved me," until they walk away. The acupressure points I use to prevent nausea obviously lack side effects. I concocted a blend of essential oils to combat post-operative nausea, but didn't offer it to patients until a similar commercial product hit the market. In an office setting, a similar scenario would be encouraging probiotic foods and supplements for your patients.

Honestly, the job market really matters more than anything I say in this chapter. Find helpful resources for your profession. This doesn't need to be as obvious as paying the several hundred dollar yearly membership fee for your official organization. That decision may depend on how much of an education budget you are allotted. Knowing statistics such as average salary and geographic employment differences will help guide your search. Start early so you're not interviewing in a panic while applying for boards. Who knows, maybe you'll get some tuition help out of it. If the market is soft when you graduate, just get a job wherever you can find one and deal with it. I wasn't sure about a place I worked for as an agency nurse, so I obtained permission from the anesthesia department to look around the OR the next time I worked there. Being there "unofficially" was certain to yield more information than a formal tour and interview would. Of course, I worked night shift, and the OR staff wasn't too pleased when I tagged along for an emergency surgery. Besides surly staff members (night shift is great for discovering what a place is *really* like), I met the oldest anesthesia machines I'd ever seen, which was another negative for me. It looked like a prop from a Frankenstein movie! The medications or equipment available at a hospital or group should only be a minor detail, but sometimes it can be a clue to how the department is run (or what their finances are like). "Futureproof" isn't just a technology term; there's no sense working for a company about to go bankrupt. Starting your own group would obviously pay the most but is the riskiest option by far, followed by working for a small office or a company contracted by the hospital. Becoming a hospital employee is traditionally the most stable option (especially compared to a new group with few employees) but sometimes pays less than a group. Small groups often have more expensive insurance and benefits, so stay healthy!

The guarantee of a pension from a small group isn't quite the same as a better paycheck from a large hospital. It's difficult to compare different offers, but pay attention to what your health insurance covers and how many years you have to work before money contributed to your retirement is yours to keep. If they contribute their portion once yearly, you won't have the benefit of compound interest from contributions twice a month.

The granting of an official interview is almost always a necessary step to compare packages. The exception is if you convince a clinical site to change a few letters on your badge and start paying you for the spectacular services you render. However, for most of us the process is strikingly similar to submitting information in hopes of being interviewed by our school of choice. This is why it helps to make as many connections as possible to network with people. A friend's recommendation will be taken more seriously than an impressive curriculum vitae.

I called hospital operators and convinced them to patch me through to the anesthesia department, but that particular scheme usually came to an abrupt end when I interrupted someone's lunch break. My next approach was to google anesthesia groups, which usually revealed a decrepit website built in 1998. During the interview process, you should also do a web search on yourself to make sure there are no youthful indiscretions trapped in the sticky fibers of the world wide web. That probably means I should make my band's Myspace private, or at least take down my original music video "You Can't Spell Uranium without Iran". No one wants to hire a lunatic.

How is your profession perceived by the other staff? Take two not really hypothetical hospitals. One was founded by nurses and based on a "team of equals" philosophy where everyone was addressed by their first names. The other was founded by doctors and therefore more traditional. Equality is more in your favor if you're on the lower end of the totem pole as opposed to a doctor, who may prefer the second hospital as long as the power structure wasn't too awkward or rigid. Will you be micromanaged by senior members of a physician group, or abandoned to figure things out on your own? Obviously either extreme isn't ideal for most people, but "abandoned" to one person might mean "autonomous" to another. As the new guy, let your more experienced colleagues establish the respect your profession merits. You shouldn't be the one going up to the boss with new proposals to make the schedule more efficient or telling the surgeons that you'll need to comment on their suture choice if they find issues with the anesthesia. It's not that your new perspective isn't useful, especially if you've had several different clinical experiences to compare, but limit that to your own personal advantage at first. Your perspective might be dead wrong, anyway. As a new resident or nurse, it can be difficult to differentiate between evidence-based care and the traditions of your colleagues and facility. That's why you need to be current on the literature if your training is at odds with how they do things at the new job. I'm currently writing an article for a nursing magazine about the barriers to implementing evidence-based care instead of the traditional policies and procedures put in place by administrators and managers far removed from the clinical setting. Try to find a place where innovation is rewarded instead of stifled, but like I said, consider keeping all your bright ideas to yourself until you get to know your coworkers. Oh, don't worry if you don't have any bright ideas. It's much easier to conform to the rank and file majority rather than constantly being the creative clinician sticking out like a sore thumb (and occasionally causing headaches for the poor coworkers that have to work with him). I've gotten much better at being uniform when I know I'll be relieved by a clinician who might not appreciate a Sufenta and propofol infusion as much as I do. It's a true safety issue too, if someone assuming care of your patients isn't familiar with your excellent, safe, but obviously unique techniques.

You'll be respected more for calling for help than for struggling—no matter how you look, don't sacrifice patient safety for your ego. Overconfidence leads to mistakes. In my anesthesia rotations, I was the best clinically during the middle of my rotations. At a new place, my skills would slip a little as I familiarized myself with new people, equipment, charting, and procedures, and my last weeks at a place I often mistakenly thought I'd already mastered the nuances of a facility.

Earlier I mentioned that nurses wherever I worked seemed to complain the same amount, regardless of their actual situations. Don't be a whiner—did you really just work so hard to obtain your degree just to complain about how bad you have it? I've added an extra chapter on finances because so many people work so hard for that degree only to be in the same financial position, other than exchanging a Ford for a Lexus. For RNs in particular, one wrong move or statement can confirm that "they don't teach these new millennial nurses like they used to." Especially in the OR, anything interesting you say, whether intentional or not, is fuel for the gossip inferno. Maybe at your place of work it's a warm, friendly inferno that only occasionally feeds off unfairness and perceived inequality.

So much time is wasted on petty issues like making sure no one got a day off that you were refused. There's no sense in switching your schedule and sacrificing your time off work to make people like you. It reminds me of Jeremy Lin (who everyone will have forgotten about by the time I get around to publishing this book) recalling how he used to pass out food at lunch time to make friends at school. I promise, I'm not watching ESPN again while writing; you have my full attention. I don't even have cable. That probably doesn't surprise you. Rather than buying people off with schedule changes or free Asian food, at all levels of your education and employment, be nice to your coworkers/competitors. Befriend them, especially ones who started around the same time you did. However, when you're in the OR or performing procedures, conserve that effort to focus on your new role. This may mean that your sparkling personality will be more subdued as you concentrate on your performance. Obviously, you don't want to be labeled as a quiet and moody person if you're actually chatty and cheery outside of work (but not cheerful, as we've already discussed), and there's no need to keep as low of a profile as you did as a student. Unfortunately, the general rule of flying under the radar still exists. The head of your department won't be relieved to hear that you defended all the nurse practitioners or residents when you got in that argument with a belligerent nurse—they just want peace.

Why settle for an uneasy truce though? Healthcare shouldn't be like business and retail—your coworkers aren't going to get bonuses for having more sales! We are all on the same team, and if not, the patients can sense it. As you get to know people, don't forget that we are freer with our words when we're concentrating on something else. Trying to make sure your date isn't a psychopath bent on world domination? Ask her questions while she's driving and you'll be amazed at the valuable information you gain. Similarly, shut up until you thread that epidural catheter or deliver that baby before chatting up your new friends.

I will also shut up as I've run out of clinical topics to chat you up about, dearest reader. I hope this simple guide has been of some use to you. If not, I don't want to hear about it. Just kidding, you can defame my name as freely as you'd like. I'll sell more copies that way. Once you reach your terminal degree, just remember that there are few opportunities that will make as much money as simply clocking in and out every day. There is freedom in knowing that and satisfaction in having expertise positively affecting patients. One of my classmates died a few weeks before we all passed our boards and became CRNAs. We mourned the futility of his last few years until our program directors gently corrected us. Although he never achieved his goal, our friend still relieved pain and comforted fears for so many patients. That is the true standard by which success and failure should be measured. Not by accolades or paychecks or advanced degrees, but by the human lives we have touched as health care providers.

Relationships

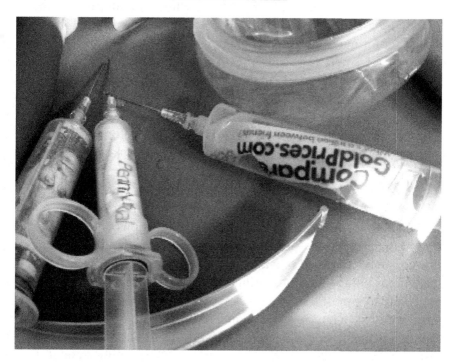

Cura te Ipsum

X. As in ex. So many clinicians have one, but I was still surprised to discover that, according to Zippia, nurse anesthetists rank twentieth in the nation for divorce rates early in life. Doesn't it seem counterintuitive that the driven, successful, caring, trustworthy, and financially secure cream of the nursing crop would be such failures at relationships? I didn't see "Fry Cook" on that list of divorcing occupations, or "Sanitation Engineer" or even "Self Employed, Which Really Means I Occasionally Con New Friends into Buying a Vial of Overpriced Essential Oils or Host Pay per View Parties for MMA Fights at my House and Pretend it's a Job." Actually, I know a dude who did the latter while his wife went to school and worked overtime as a surgical tech—they're not together any more.

I'll share a lot of websites like the above statistic in these chapters, none of which I currently have a financial relationship with. Like footnotes, few if any are worth stopping for until you finish the book and therefore have nothing else to look forward to in life. This isn't a collection of blog posts clumsily clumped together, so they're not integral. As with the chapter on clinical skills, it's important for me to be knowledgeable and thorough. This is why this material is here (and after the "About the Author" section in the Kindle version) instead of cutely segued into one of the much shorter chapters before it. I will end the <3 and $ chapters with descriptions of additional resources you may find useful at a later date. The topic of relationships for caregivers will be life changing for a few of you and perhaps harmless drivel for those who'd rather skip ahead to the finance section.

So is the problem that we're perfectionists and can't tolerate mistakes? Is it pride, or lack of effort? Rather than treat them rhetorically, let me answer those important questions one at a time. Part of the problem lies in the narrow focus from trying too hard, as if love can be mastered like a thoracic epidural. We all need meticulous clinical abilities at this level, but personality tests are a good way to honestly assess our level of neuroticism and understand those we love. They're fun, and unlike the MMPI screening for multiple personalities and psychosis, your loved one won't be insulted if you suggest them. I mentioned 16personalities.com (in part because it doesn't demand your email address and beg you to buy things) and similar tests earlier. This chapter is slightly more informative for men because we tend to prefer succinylcholine without propofol to books on relationships, as opposed to my female readers who browsed every "10 Ways to Know if you or your Partner is Terrible" article available at the first hint of trouble. So, a personality resource that also takes fashion and beauty into account is liveyourtruth.com. With the exception of my other works (none of which cost more than a kid's hot chocolate at Starbucks), I don't recommend necessarily purchasing the resources mentioned in this book. Rather, by surveying the free insights they offer, you can see what fits and move on to the next expert without getting trapped in an inevitably narrow and pricey system to achieve success.

Knowing yourself is the first step, because even interpreting the actions of others is impossible without comprehension of your own motives, beliefs, and ways to give and receive love. It's like getting on the field without knowing the sport or rules—not going to score a lot of points that way. Truth and transparency are vital for any intimate relationship, including the one with yourself. Clicking on the quizzes on 5lovelanguages.com is an excellent beginning to understand your own anger, ability to forgive and appreciate, and the most efficient ways to feel loved. Yes, efficient. With endless time on your side, patients would do great, relationships would flourish, compound interest would be magical—but most of us must squish high quality interactions and care into a very full schedule. It could be that you are generally tolerant of imperfection, but work or school stress alters your natural inclinations. The ability to "turn off" hyper vigilance without compartmentalizing to the point of burying parts of yourself requires introspection. A less complex way to state my point is, "Check yourself before you wreck yourself." Ask those you love for help. One huge reason for writing this chapter is that my career as a caregiver gave me the ability to place each emotion in a separate box and turn empathy on and off like a switch. Some of my co-workers struggle with the overpowering urge to take care of everyone in their life. Alternatively, if precise control of vital signs and the satisfaction of seeing immediate results by pushing a syringe worsens your OCD, it may be time to work on weaknesses instead of embracing personality factors that make critical care so appealing.

I originally intended to avoid clinical examples in this chapter, so readers could pass it off to their significant other to read and understand what they're going through. Solid plan, but it's much more productive to improve the relationship by fixing yourself rather than the attitude of, "Wow, they really need to read this." We don't choose strengths and weaknesses for ourselves or others. Think right now of the most annoying habit possessed by the person you love most on this earth. Some of you have a lot of work to do because you are thinking of your precious cat missing the litter box.

Anyway, all that effort just to change a quality initially perceived as a positive trait (eg, "She's so fun and goofy," or, "He is so well organized"). Everyone has weaknesses. Accept that you can't have well behaved children, financial freedom, a sizzling romance, and serious social media game. As the band Sanctus Real sings, "Everyone wants everyone else's everything." Something will always be lacking—don't make it contentment. Your weakness will never be a strength. Work on it and improve yourself, because sole focus on increasing competence at what you're best at leads to incompleteness, but strike a healthy balance between understanding and improving yourself. That balance means lies somewhere between, "This is just who I am," and "We would make it if I could only make my man more sympathetic or make myself more aggressive."

This story likely has the longevity of Dwight Howard's trade from the Orlando Magic mentioned earlier, but right now Google is in the news for firing an employee who pointed out that female disinterest in computer programming and other STEM jobs may be due to biology rather than oppression. Any chances for accurate details of the story were lost several days ago in the typical onslaught from both sides to craft a narrative that exalted their beliefs and demonized any opposition. Before I venture deeper into this touchy topic, my answer to the question of, "Can I tolerate mistakes?" is, "Yes, if a firm sense of identity and boundaries are in place to avoid enabling, we actually all need to be more accommodating to those we love." This issue actually deals with the nurses (three this week, in fact) who tell me, "Healthcare has changed so much and isn't nearly as fun as it was when we were underpaid and overworked twenty years ago. Then, we were a team who could nurture and heal patients and had the freedom to do what mattered."

Dr. John Gray, author of *Men are from Mars, Women are from Venus*, believes that much of female unhappiness in today's relationships and the reason that they initiate the majority of divorces is because they don't have enough time to be freely female. They find it difficult to transition after coming home from "man jobs" that require logic and defined goals instead of support from other females, interpersonal skills, cooperation, and freedom of expression. A woman may sort out her feelings during an argument while a man is more likely to concentrate on solutions and decisions.

Comparatively, nursing has changed from "take care of the patient, relieve their suffering, and be their advocate" to "fulfill this list of five things so the hospital doesn't lose money, and make sure to spend a lot of time charting specific tasks you did rather than help out your coworkers and build a cohesive team." Older male nurses reminisce about those "good old days" much less. Maybe because they didn't like wearing the white hats and hose—I digress. I think Gray's work on gender roles generalizes too broadly, but I will incorporate some of it, especially regarding conflict.

During stressful times like anesthesia school or transitioning to a new phase in our lives (such as locums anesthesia), we are more likely to revert to our basic instincts and primal roots—the amygdala and "fight or flight" response—rather than rational, long term decision making. Emotions increase and logic decreases. Because I've seen what alternative medicine can do for mood disorders, I have strong feelings against the chronic use of anti-anxiety meds and antidepressants as a first line therapy, but I am all for them in the midst of making calm, reasonable decisions when the world is falling apart. That's a lot more rational than, "Living with her was a black hole, so I had to escape before doing anything else." Everything we do gets infected with irrationality and unpredictability as we seek to defend ourselves. As I've said in speeches, just trying to keep these feeble patients alive triggers our reptilian brain with its rudimentary needs. Be on your guard and accept this now, before you wake up next to a "friend" in the call room or linen closet.

The second question I mentioned, "Is it pride?" makes me think of a two year old refusing to flush away the glorious creation their gut made out of animal crackers and goldfish. Despite my snark, I think the world of you, sympathize with the incredible challenges of sustaining deep, meaningful connections with people during stressful times, and do not assume you're an arrogant jerk. Though much of this chapter challenges the notion of doing what's best for you at all costs, suffering silently is not a realistic solution. As surely as our tissues prefer oxygen to nitrogen, we all have pride, whether it's overt or masquerades as some sort of dutiful humble brag. Some of my worst anesthesia students were prideful, and it hindered them from growth and change. Welcome transformation clinically and in relationships. For a chill person like me, that uncomfortable feeling is the only way to deduce I'm learning through challenges. The answer to pride in ourselves or others can be to have clear boundaries, which are a defensive shield, not a controlling, offensive weapon. This clarifies what we're not willing to accept, but more often the solution is accommodation—letting people be themselves instead of the construct that most fulfills *you*.

The reason for my tangent on personality types was that most people don't know themselves well enough to articulate their needs, causing an awkward situation when a significant other manages to finally give them what they want, and it has little relevance to actual needs. I haven't met an anesthesia student yet who wants to arrive in an OR before six o'clock and set up for multiple cases, but that experience helps them not forget crucial equipment when they have to prepare in a hurry. I would encourage my senior students to roll in two or three hours after six, since they'd already mastered the fine art of attaching stickers to syringes and laryngoscope blades to handles, but by that point they were usually too dutiful to slack off without feeling guilty.

Unfortunately, even those prone to serving others at all cost don't get a free pass. Several comedians have made careers out of explaining how their Italian/Jewish/Greek, etc. mothers reveled in being a martyr. Although Dr. Ed Young remarks that hoping the other person will make you happy results in two ticks and no dog, sometimes people continue to give because it feels safer and more comfortable than receiving. Instead of thinking that I'm better than this, self-righteousness for unjust suffering becomes a pious identity rooted in the pride of, "Look what an amazing person I am to put with all this crap." It is absolutely true that some of the personalities from the tests mentioned do get their jollies from helping others, but that just scratches the surface of compatibility. Finding someone authentic, with character and actions that match their motivations and beliefs, supersedes matching yourself with an introvert, or a funny and friendly person, or even someone who seems to share your values. Without consistency and openness, you'll struggle to even recognize what the other person wants and needs for fulfillment. The ability to say, "I am wrong, I'm sorry, and I'm going to behave differently now," is a quality that should be sought out much more than, "We have the exact same political beliefs about gender issues and spiritual beliefs about everything else." Anyone can vaguely apologize for past behavior, but pinpoint actions that need to change today despite good intentions.

The final question regarding insecurity and selfishness is,

"Where does my self worth come from, and does it fluctuate?" The Latin phrase titling this section is the Aramaic proverb, "Physician, heal thyself," an ancient version of, "Hold my beer, I've got this." That's exactly what we try to do by promoting growth and progress at all cost. I have a friend who knows he is too rigid, but he gets uptight about not chilling out sufficiently. I have no idea what that feels like, but I've caught myself becoming apathetic about my failure to stop being laid back. Good ol' fashioned selfishness exposes itself much more readily than lack of self, which decays relationships with subtle slowness. We don't know how to accept gifts; to bask in "good enough" without feeling we have to earn love and respect from those we love, or success from the world by continual effort and optimal performance.

It's natural to feel good about yourself because you provide for your family and even serve those in need, but what happens in the inevitable situation where you don't measure up, or others fail to express gratitude for what you've done? Most of us lash out in anger, or even worse, implode inward and see ourselves as unworthy failures. I remember telling a despondent SRNA, "Yes, you couldn't find the hole where air goes in and out and I had to intubate the patient for you, but this has nothing to do with how good of a provider you are, or your anesthesia knowledge, or even how you're going to perform clinically or intellectually for the rest of this surgery. You will still do great, because your identity doesn't come from messing up a mechanical skill at the very beginning of this case, just like my value doesn't depend on me remembering this conversation and writing it down so people will know I am the wisest, most encouraging CRNA ever." Just kidding about that last part. My worth won't change whether this new update really takes off or if I continue to sell one book a month.

We must find deeper roots to affirm unchanging value, because performance is only based on your last anesthetic or what you did for your girlfriend yesterday. For me, it's my faith in God and His love that never leaves me or hesitates, even when I walk through circumstances that would dry up the coffers of all the televangelists advocating spirituality as a crutch to avoid hardship. My beliefs work for me because they existed before times of despair, as opposed to the Pitocin-prodded, pill-popping preggo who decides to have a natural pregnancy once she's in the hospital. You know, like the Facebook friends who get religion and prattle on about Jesus or the Buddha only during a hard break up. Find an unconditional, sustainable source for value; comfort and respect that flows naturally without striving for worthiness or spending thousands on "self care."

Valuing yourself means that no one else is responsible for your reactions or emotional well-being. To paraphrase Greg Smalley, there may be times that you must tell loved ones, "You're not being careful with my heart, and it's my job to not let it be treated with disrespect, so I'm going to put boundaries between us until it's safe." Don't rely on others to always remember the right way to treat you. That's my whole point in this, not some futile exercise in self esteem that fails the next time we are offended. If you only love yourself when you succeed, you will teach others to treat you the same way. As never-ending as a c. Diff patient on Lactulose's bowel movement, you'll end up jumping through the flaming hoop of performance to prove your worth and get all your needs met.

Give and Go Teamwork

So really, the "Physician, heal thyself" section you just read was about getting to know yourself better: the internal relationship between who you really are, who you want to be, and why conflicts with others sometimes arise from that difference. As I type this, I'm sheltering strangers from central Florida in my house as Hurricane Irma churns closer. It gives me the warm and fuzzies, and I realize I feel good about helping because it makes me look kind and generous. Why deny it? Sure, I'm being a good Christian, and I'm "passing it forward" and working like part of a team, but no one said my motives must be 100% pure at all times. Teamwork is our next topic, starting with this picture of my younger brother and me.

In sixth grade, I was part of the basketball team for the first time ever. I am absurdly loyal, but I should have quit, because we practiced before and after school (I was usually in a sweatshirt because my immigrant parents didn't know that American kids wear shorts and t-shirts, even in winter, if they're exercising indoors), I rarely played in games, and, most importantly, I was horrible. First off, that picture is from tenth grade, not sixth grade, and I still look like Sponge Bob could box me out. Second, I was so inept and inaccurate that anyone within ten feet of my layup attempt was in danger from the basketball hitting them in the face after careening off the bottom or top of the rim or backboard. Then in seventh grade, there were only six of us on the junior high team, and everything changed.

Actually, I was still terrible, so that didn't change. Even today one of my bios reads "enjoys playing several sports poorly." But, I cared if we won or lost, and my team needed me, so I became much better at rebounding, defending, and every other aspect of basketball that doesn't require the ball to travel from a player's hand to the rim en route to the bottom of the net. The other team no longer rejoiced when I stepped onto the court. I wasn't striving for personal achievement by scoring twenty, or even two points a game. I simply did what I could to give my team a better chance at winning. Similarly, a good soccer player doesn't strive to score 0.6 goals a game. Instead, they just create an environment to make goals more likely (even if they have to flop like a diva). Teamwork is vital in relationships, because the ball hog who does everything and the benchwarmer just enjoying a better seat than the spectators can't overcome challenges and bring home the trophy, which relates to my phrase, "Don't graduate alone."

Basic human nature reveals itself in creation stories of "first teams," as my Greek ancestors, Native Americans, and other cultures tried to explain why the world works the way it does. In the Biblical account of Adam and Eve, we find the classic choice between growth and relationship. In another context, growth is the challenging job that increases your clinical skills, while relationship is the easy unit where all your friends work and have a good time. Discomfort versus nourishment, and neither works well in isolation. I think that by biting into the forbidden fruit, Eve chose growth—the ability to know both good and evil and become more like God, even at the expense of equality with her husband. By choosing to also disobey God's command not to eat from that tree, Adam chose relationship—joining his wife in an unwise choice rather than abstaining. We can clearly see that abandoning your teammate for the sake of personal growth (our culture's preferred choice) or wallowing in enabling behavior to save the relationship both end in disaster. Relationship compromises often result in two unhappy people instead of one. We create false dichotomies to make the lesser evil more appealing, but there is often a balanced option between choosing only growth or relationship. Like most humans today when caught in the act, Adam and Eve tried to deflect by activating the blame cycle, accusing each other and the devil.

It's human nature to let go of responsibility if we are unhappy in a relationship, or to take on more roles if we are trying to salvage it. Both are mistakes. Maybe you need to receive more rather than give more. Taking a subservient role because she is more successful or he is more attractive also leads to imbalance. The "lesser" person needs to find important responsibilities for their partner to combat the superficial message society sends of, "They could do better than you." Your husband may have conflicting feelings about you being more educated than him, or you may feel like you need to be in charge since your needs are temporarily more important. Without honesty and self-examination (because, whether conscious or internalized, one perspective can only reveal part of the truth), resentment builds.

If anesthesia school isn't stressing your relationships, you're doing something wrong. You need to either start studying more or abandon a maid and butler relationship for something much more authentic that creates intimacy. Obtain balance by investing yourself fully. That balance also lessens the urge to "make up" for a partner's idiosyncrasies by one of you being sweet and the other tough; one generous and hospitable, and the other wincing at every dollar spent, etc. Instead of dipping up and down like a see-saw, balance requires healthy tension much like tent poles on canvas. It will ebb and flow—one partner always wants more intimacy than the other—but balance isn't two people at opposite ends of a bell curve. It's also not meeting every single need to prevent resentment from becoming fatal contempt. If you're a student's spouse, I realize you can't squeeze the bag and breathe for her patients. For SRNA's, forgetting all other responsibilities to concentrate on not intubating the esophagus every day is not an option either, even for just a two year program.

One method to work as a team is to create the habit of actively cherishing each other. It takes effort to make someone feel valuable and needed. For the opposite feeling, reread what I wrote about addictions earlier. In his aptly named book, *Cherish*, Gary Thomas suggests planning something for your husband or wife akin to the Make a Wish Foundation (except for the part where they die afterwards), even if it takes years. Take turns being the organ grinder or the monkey. Warning! This is not shaping up to be one of my better analogies, but here we go. I'm not putting a dime in someone's hat if they're on a street corner cranking out tunes, but if they have a dancing monkey, I'm gonna make it rain dollar bills like a Greek wedding reception. The organ grinder is doing his best to enhance the monkey's performance, despite my lack of recognition for his…grinding. If love is my woeful junior high basketball team, then cherish is offense—putting points on the board and actively casting a partner in the best possible light. I've never seen an organ grinder say, "That's it Monkey, you're stealing the show, so this time it's my turn and I'm going to dance and you crank out the music!" Actually, I don't think that's a thing anymore—not since the invention of the phonograph or maybe eight tracks and PETA. Cherishing others is so hard for us because we prefer transactional relationships rather than competing over who can care for the other person best. Burn out results from a disillusioned hope for reciprocity. Read that again. Giving only as good as you're getting leads to that aforementioned hoop of endless performance to be accepted.

Enough sappiness for now (referring to "cherish," not the cute dancing monkey in his little red jacket with gold buttons and matching hat); let's discuss close friends. I heard a preacher the other day talk about forming a "wisdom team" of advisors with diverse experiences and knowledge for tough decisions. He used large superhero action figures as an illustration, which is where his metaphor failed. If The Hulk and Wolverine are trusted friends revered for their mental shrewdness and thoughtfulness, your wisdom team will fare as well as the first few Hulk movie reboots. That's why I often recommend trained, professional counselors rather than drinking buddies or acquaintances with good Instagram photos and four weeks of life coach training.

Bad advice is so much worse than no advice at all, just like someone in a bad relationship is three steps away from finding "the one" while a single person is one step away. If you're wondering, I'd say those steps are, 1) Break up 2) Go through the dark night of the soul 3) Find yourself in the same spot as a single person attracting someone. Although it didn't start out that way, I give a lot of interpersonal and relationship advice through my company BEHAVE Wellness, and besides my own successes and failures, I've been involved in similar projects for years, including a Facebook group called "SRNAs Moving On." However, I took Aquatic Exercise rather than the final class I needed for my psychology minor. Except for one glorious week of dodge ball and water polo, it turned out to be geriatric calisthenics in a freezing swimming pool while the diving team snickered at us. This isn't an academic exercise or book report, but I researched more than one hundred sources before writing this chapter. The prevalence of stupid advice astounded me. To be honest, relationship advice has a lot in common with the far fringes of alternative medicine and various diet shakes: anecdotal evidence of spectacular results, but even the wisest words or technique may not be suited for your individual situation. I've cast a wide net, but a competent one if you are willing to let whatever fits your situation resonate fully rather than deciding if you agree with it intellectually.

Although the two of you are the all-stars, there are other teammates, and I'm not talking about sister wives. Friends and family can lead you astray despite having your best in mind. Sometimes that's exactly why they do more harm than good. They have your best in mind rather than what's better for the relationship. Even prioritizing the other person ahead of the relationship finds us back at that same flaming hoop, competing for worth and identity. If you could do better than your current partner, the very act of leaving them like a Silicon Valley startup looking for the Next Big Thing drops you right back at their level, doesn't it? Placeholder status until something better shows up is best dealt with early, while it's still partially subconscious. Brutal honesty may sting, but conflict brings greater intimacy when a couple shares vulnerabilities. It's very common that both simultaneously feel unloved and like a burden, but it may be too late once bitterness crystallizes. The goal is not to compare effort to ensure each contributes exactly 50%, but to validate each other's perspective. Sometimes when I don't feel heard at work, I'll offer terrible ideas with a straight face to see the reaction to, "Listen, I'll just sedate the patient for the leg amputation, and it'll work out great."

Actions catch up to beliefs. Leave your favorite cable news network on for a few days and notice how you treat those with differing politics. The mark of a true friendship isn't unconditional support, but the ability to thrive while voicing opinions the other person disagrees with. Although habits and the environment are influential, you can only control yourself. Censoring loved ones makes vulnerability and authentic relationships impossible while doing little to resolve the underlying fear. Fear is underrated as a stupidity attenuation tool, but I'm talking about deep fears that likely formed in childhood. It might be fear of rejection, fear of being told what to do, or fear of incompetence, but I've found that most arguments trace back to a person's core fear. Exposing that fear to your mate and dealing with it in the open may be the hardest thing you ever do, and it's ok to do so gradually as they earn more trust. You may even find yourself resolving issues, as you are no longer trying to have a dance-off without knowing the style or hearing the music.

What about seemingly articulate friends who don't have your back? Even if both of you are sincere, don't deceive yourself and ignore ludicrous situations, like that single male nurse who sends you encouraging emails every morning and prays with you every night as you grapple with your relationship problems. A lion should never ask a vulture or hyena if he's full or needs a few more bites of zebra. No matter how wise, objective, or rational their answer, they still benefit from the lion leaving the carcass. As a successful person, there will always be sharks surrounding you, waiting for opportunity and vulnerability. And zebra—sharks get zebra so rarely that it's considered a delicacy. As Steve Harvey loves to tell women, "He's your friend, because that's all you'll let him be." It's natural to find comfort in unloading your troubles into the sympathetic ear of a coworker during stressful times, but even if you don't wake up together in the call room the next morning, it resembles the thought, "I'm sure I can just light one of these trees on fire to give me warmth, but control the situation so I don't engulf this dry forest in flames."

So what should you do with pride, unmet needs and the feeling that you deserve more? I've already told you that side chicks are out. Calculating what you deserve is an endless distraction. My pediatric trauma patients don't deserve to die with their bodies filleted open as we frantically try to find the source of internal bleeding. This goes against popular culture, but being on a team means you don't always get your share of met needs. Voltaire said, "To enjoy life, we must touch much of it lightly." That's everything. My need of scoring ten points a game went unmet in junior high because it would have taken me twenty, maybe forty shot attempts to achieve that goal. A relationship centered on meeting needs, even vital ones, will flourish until the first need inevitably goes unmet. I trained my brain for anesthesia school by having one super critical patient in ICU I was completely responsible for on Monday, and ten patients on a medical floor on Tuesday. Instead of meeting all my patient's needs on Tuesday, I had to prioritize those that mattered most considering the length of my shift, and ignore other needs, even though they were legitimate. Making hard choices is part of adulting. According to marriage researcher John Gottman, marital unhappiness tends to be transient, and most relational conflicts don't even have a solution. Choose today to have joy in life despite not having everything work out the way you would prefer.

Community and Intimacy

Community is most relevant to single folks who stuck around for the jokes. I'm still laughing at the organ grinder analogy, and I wrote it yesterday! No, I take that back, I'm actually laughing at my penile block joke. I'll probably lose you joke lovers a few chapters from now when I try to explain useful technology to nurses deciding whether to apply to anesthesia school. Although a bad relationship is excruciatingly lonely, married life does come with a built in buddy—it's written between the lines in the marriage vows that they should be amusing and hang out. That need for safe, supportive companionship—not the hyenas and vultures feeding off of your success or waiting for you to slip up—is universal regardless of personality type, love language, or sexual orientation. Your ferret and a good book with a glass of wine doesn't cut it. As an extrovert who relishes transactional, shallow friendships, I slowly realized that although it was fun to write skits for acquaintances who would then play sports with me, I was wasting time I could spend pursuing real community.

The apostle Paul recommended that the Corinthian community stay married or single rather than try to change their status. Most scholars believe he based his advice on the reality of intense stress and persecution in Corinth—similar to graduate school, but with exciting gladiator matches instead of passive-aggressive student evaluations. Divorce is a nuisance—ain't nobody got time for that between clinicals, studying for boards, and trying to stay out of the hospital rumor mill. The same can be said for forming relationships, but I'm well aware that it gets harder and harder to find decent friends, much less lovers, as we age. Kindling a friendship requires spending plenty of time together on purpose, like in a study group. Work doesn't count. I have to be at work or I won't have money, and even after eight years at my primary job, put a gun to my head and ask, "What's that nurse's name?" and I'll say, "Uh, she's about sixty-five, so probably Judy, Trudy, or Sharon."

For some, my dire warning about shacking up with friends in the linen closet sounds great, as long as you don't wake up to Judy, Trudy, and Sharon. If those three still sound fun, please consider therapy and the Phenergan regional block mentioned fifty pages back. Or perhaps you feel so secure in your current relationship that the concept is too improbable to guard against. We all have times of vulnerability. A recovering alcoholic tends to reach back for the bottle during difficult times, and addiction leers most menacingly when there is little under our control. Why else would playing the hero in a video game all day be so compelling, if in real life paying Mom rent for the basement on time was the most heroic event of the month? You may have contingency plans to make sure it's all harmless fun and no one gets hurt. Maybe they're effective. One of the reasons I wrote this chapter was several workplaces where anesthetists had to be shuffled so "Ex-Wife A" didn't have to work near "Awkward Stalker B" or interact with "Affair Partner C" near "Meddling Anesthesiologist D" and "Only that One Harmless Time a Long Time Ago but I Still Can't Look them in the Eye E."

Stress and misfortune bond people, so coworkers or classmates may form a tight-knit community just like hostages would. Although initially supportive, in extreme cases it can get very dark. Students have told me, "This preceptor at a clinical site picked me, but to increase my chance of getting good evaluations and graduating, they want sex." Focus on realities and priorities outside the bubble of a toxic and belittling environment. Since you only see them at weddings and funerals, you wouldn't treat extended relatives better than your spouse, even for the sake of peace on Thanksgiving. You're a team, and there are very few battles better fought alone, even the awkward ones. Thinking that it will only be temporary, sometimes we call upon the ones we go home to every day to endure the greatest sacrifices.

Although I don't bring problems from home with me, my coworkers see the worst side of me, so I can save the best parts of me for those I love the most, rather than taking out pent up anger on them. I mean, I'm still funny and nice and do my job, but why be the most patient, swallow-injustice-without-a-word type of person for those who are trying to use your skills to make as much money as possible? Part of having boundaries is telling other adults things that are uncomfortable and they might not want to hear, but won't hurt them. I realize this issue hinges on the financial ability to leave a job, which we'll discuss in Chapter $. Grace for failing like every human does should be extended the most to those you choose to live life with. You may spend more time with fellow residents, as in the quotation below, but you didn't choose them.

"The House of God was known for its progressiveness, especially in relation to the way it treated its House Staff. It was one of the first hospitals to offer free marital counseling, and when that failed, to encourage divorce. On average, during their stay, about 80% of the married medically qualified Sons and Daughters would make use of this suggestion, separate from their spouses, and take up with some bombshell from Private Doctors, House Administration, Nursing, Patients, Social Service, Telephone and Beeper Operators, and Housekeeping."

Those immortal words were penned in Samuel Shem's sentinel work *House of God* almost four decades before I ever wrote a medical satire article for "GomerBlog" or "The Twerk Vaccine," but they still hold true today. SRNA school is uniquely stressful to relationships because there's less prestige then a medical residency coupled with high graduate school tuition—the injustice of paying money to be treated badly while making money for someone else. Essentially though, there's nothing new going on here. Yes, people split up in anesthesia school, but they also do between high school and college, in the military, and at any other life juncture powerful enough to redefine identity.

I am much less hilarious today than I was ten years ago, because with the exception of this book, I'm at a stage in life where humor doesn't get me as far. My core personality hasn't outgrown zaniness and immaturity, but those traits are (slightly) less pronounced. If I were a woman with two children running around in diapers, I would want an organized team player for a husband, not a comedian. A middle-aged couple with kids out of the house could once again appreciate an exciting, empathetic mate rather than a practical and stable one, but each stage of life will require something different. Adapt or stagnate, and in medicine, there's another name for the scenario where the ebb and flow of life is resisted: gangrene. Your resistance could be based on false assumptions about yourself or the idea that, "Life would be perfect if they _____ instead of _____."
You are responsible only for changing yourself, although many marriage counselors (mainly Divorce Busters) believe that going at it alone and indirectly changing others is possible just by altering your habitual reactions and responses. Rather than getting stuck in the rut of either enabling or always taking, realize that interactions are circular: she did this and I did that and she did that, rather than a linear cause and effect of she forgot to buy organic, free range

almond milk so I got mad and yelled at her. We teach others how to treat us.

So if school or residency is consuming enough to reshape personalities, it's natural to think that the same determination and process to succeed in that environment will work in other areas too. We sweat, fret, pray, and pay attention to every word the other person says, unknowingly filtering every action and reaction through the flawed perceptions that got us to the troubled phase of "working on the relationship." Works about as well as turning down cheesecake for a plate of raw cauliflower, right? They're both off-white, starch containing foods that will probably give you bad gas, but that dramatic substitution isn't going to work out. So why do we think that the ability to be at ease and effortlessly connect with someone who makes us feel love and laughter can be recreated with anxiety and homework?

Whether you're trying to get an ex back, forget a previous lover, or, more commonly, safeguard the relationship you do have during perilous times, the key is emotional connection. Even the strongest relationships require vigilance—you wouldn't try to intubate a challenging patient without a backup plan, or neglect checking the blood sugar of a patient on an insulin drip because she looked like she was doing fine. Emotional connection is adding openness and honor (a combination akin to peanut butter and chocolate) to Gary Chapman's famous love languages, along with the completely unique ways that a loved one interprets intimacy. With the ability to speak heart to heart to another human, no impediment can separate you. Without that deep connection, the excuse for why it's not working out will fluctuate, but the result will be the same. Few actions warm the heart more than grace and forgiveness instead of keeping a record of wrongs. Much more grace can be easily extended to another person if both are being their authentic selves. Rather than being tied to a specific outcome, that's how healthy relationships start. It's the thrill of, "Let's see where this goes" as two real people connect. I've never fallen for anyone without first being able to relax and enjoy them for who they are.

Think of the marriage altar as that sacrificial place where fun times are slaughtered for the sake of the relationship. What better way to please your partner than to show that they are number one? Actually, it's a lot like the person with back pain who thinks, "Well, if I give up golf, my back will feel better." The lack of movement makes the pain worse, and the sacrifices keep coming as their quality of life decreases. Selfishness should be sacrificed, but not personhood and everything enjoyable. We start piling up all these sacrifices and don't notice that one of the items is our very essence. Hygiene issues and anaerobic metabolism instead of the Krebs Cycle aside, no one wants to date a zombie. Regardless of your philosophical bent, surely in this enlightened age we seek intimacy, not appeasement as if to some god who must be placated to assure bountiful harvest. "Oh, sacrificing my children on the molten hands of Molech still wasn't enough? Let me create a graven image of your likeness out of Gouda cheese." Your first mistake was not picking a harder cheese such as cheddar.

So, don't give up every hobby and friend just because the career keeps you busy and leftover time should be given to your partner. They will be initially overjoyed, but you won't resemble the person with a rich, full life who attracted them in the first place. If only one person meets all the needs in your life, boundary issues exist. Men often do need time to recharge before taking on the task of making sure their spouses feel fulfilled emotionally—something that for most present-day women is no longer available from their community of friends. If you're already rolling your eyes and thinking the words, "heteronormative gender constructs" at my attempt to increase understanding, consider how unsatisfied today's seemingly successful women are with their relationship and financial status. Remember, I'm trying to give relevant guidance more than conventional, spectacular advice. Especially if they're still operating from a "needs" mindset, pleasing a woman is goal number one to a man, which is why, "I just can't make her happy" is such a bitter complaint. Hiding alone in a man cave watching several three hour football games a week is not a justifiable way to regroup, so focus on quality activities that give your mind a quick break. That way you can truly relax instead of feeling angry eyes boring into your skull from the next room.

According to John Gray, women can relax when the men in their lives show compassion and care about the issues they talk about without trying to solve problems. This can require some dodging and ducking to not get defensive or respond to seemingly unfair accusations. Defensiveness and justification defeats the whole purpose of letting a woman open up and feel better just by talking about frustrations. It isn't about accuracy, because most men won't feel better by talking something out unless a partner agrees with their conclusions. She will be less angry if she feels she has a right to be and has a safe place to process her emotions and discover how she really feels. Invalidating rebuttals or frustration from him stops this oral journaling process. Keeping a diary may help some women, but it's not a substitute for feeling supported when expressing themselves to others.

Although most women really want their man to be vulnerable and share more, this may cover their own hidden need to be supported, sensitive, and open. As he opens up into some sort of warrior princess, sharing his most vulnerable issues, she can eventually lose attraction to that because she doesn't know what to do with it and hesitates to burden him with her own problems. Some of these gender differences might not apply to your current relationship. When present, they may stem from powerlessness and not receiving forgiveness, acceptance, and appreciation as a child. This results in his feminine side reminding him of problems and his male side being unable to solve them. Alternatively, the woman perceives many more problems than the man, but feels the burden to solve them all. Anesthesia school is emasculating for a man whether he attends or she does. He needs her to comment on what he does do right, even if that requires fishing for compliments, to prevent the implosion from needless sacrificial behavior mentioned above (or explosion from blatantly selfish behavior).

So how does he bond, then, if not by sharing feelings? Women unwind and feel nurtured by accepting comfort from a trusted source, but men love being useful. He might want to fix an old car during down time, while she might want a massage or a mini vacation. Because I'm all about bioavailable mineral absorption, I take Epsom salt baths frequently, but the thought hasn't ever crossed my mind, "I need a bath bomb, lavender essential oil, and a lot more bubbles in this tub." I had a friend pull up to a crack house in the hood because they advertised the cheapest massage on Craigslist. I can easily see myself doing that, but not any women I know. Males bond by successfully doing. This goes back to the video game that spawned a revolution after the demise of Atari: Mario wants to win Princess Peach's admiration by rescuing her from Bowser.

Competing with other males, playing sports for exercise, and recharging when necessary rather than feeling guilty for needing time alone are ways for men to heal themselves in a toxic world.

Something as simple as watching an action movie with a friend may be all the time away they need. Ingratiating behavior doesn't nurture the male soul, but take a spa day and find out for yourself, because the underlying research is wide open for interpretation. In contrast to taking alone time when he doesn't feel like talking, if a man sees something that needs to be done, he should do it immediately to get in touch with his masculine side. Generosity is part of that, even if not appreciated appropriately. Purely transactional actions aren't generous anyway. Relax with hardship: stay masculine (and by that I mean your truer self, not some toxic, insecure bravado) by pushing yourself. Feel the fear and do it anyway. I did this at more relaxed clinical sites to increase my skill at unconventional approaches to anesthesia. You don't want to fall into, "This is a really fragile patient, so let me try something I've never done before."

An easy way to spot inauthentic masculinity is the presence of ridiculousness. My belligerent patient today threatened the male nurse, who used to play professional rugby, while only having kind words for me and my jaw-dropping140 pound frame. I tactfully pointed out that his surgery would make it difficult to beat anyone up for quite some time, and that I was trying very hard not to laugh at him. Instead of embracing his current vulnerability and walking through his fear, my patient was crying and whining one minute, trash talking the next, and making a fool out of himself for literally hours.

The theme here seems to be that self-control is essential to manhood and expression central to femininity. This view has its limitations, else we end up with bottled up, frustrated men or petulant women, but there is a grain of truth in Gray's stereotypes. Taking care of business by setting goals and dependably achieving them shows leadership, while inconsistent control over anger or lust shows through in men bullying others to act tough or looking at porn every time they're alone. Men, express anger when needed, but in a firm, clear voice rather than vague shouting that only communicates weakness. This is especially important in the stiff hierarchy of healthcare. That anger often comes from being taken for granted, while hers may be rooted in feeling minimized. During conflict, this leads to pain and vulnerability. The struggle during those times is to access love.

Can her heart remain open? Can he care for her through his pain? And if they can't deliver and disappoint us, can we develop patience and hunker down until the storm passes, or are we back to the analogy of trying to light just one tree on fire without burning the forest? Thoughtful insights rarely come while escaping death via immolation. Reflexive, amygdala-based survival skills take priority at the exact moment we could really use articulate communication instead of defensiveness. Instead of one partner taking one step back or two forward, both might pull back. That's where leniency comes in, and interpreting the partnership. Is it cooperation toward the same goal, or each having a portion under their control? I haven't included many exercises in this book (because they're boring), but a helpful one in this case, especially if you lack a great support system, is to write out the critical blame you want to smear your partner with.

Respond to that first letter to yourself by writing another where they say what you want to hear, and finally write a third letter of forgiveness back to them. Make it specific to their mistakes, but the whole exercise should only take a few minutes. There is greater suffering from not forgiving if you also love that person. Obviously, giving them that third letter with a noble, "Look how forgiving I am" is a poor idea, as is reading anything that your partner wrote privately to clear their thoughts. Forgive, but acknowledge the truth. No one deserves to be treated like they treated you. This is skill deficiency instead of blame. After all, it's not your fault if you can't get an epidural the first time you try on a writhing pregnant woman's back.

The above is not a long term solution, as the other person doesn't know how you feel. Suppressing negative feelings weakens the ability to feel in general. Basing decisions on emotions leads to inconsistency that prevents others from understanding us or trusting enough to receive love. Feelings *do* provide insight to solving problems. He occasionally needs to feel he can do no wrong, and she must have the safety to get upset and sort out feelings without judgment. Channel those feelings into a common purpose rather than the ever elusive search for happiness. This allows the male to give and feel useful and respected. In turn, the female receives and feels cherished rather than like a second mother trying to teach her man table manners and also how to lead her.

Cut your Losses

86

Perpetual butterflies dive-bomb your stomach, until one day they flutter into your thoracic cavity and out the gaping hole where your heart once beat joyfully, and everything is dead like the stillness of winter. Stop posting about rising from the ashes like a phoenix. Sit with your grief. Those who never get over failing anesthesia school, or the divorce, or the death, often try to detour around grief. That leads to never-ending tea with the Mad Hatter until someone stuffs them into a teapot and they have to face it anyway, at a place and time not of their choosing. Walking through pain and despair purposefully, at the right time, means you can rely on the support system that may not understand completely, but is there for you. The alternative—finding some rebound love, for example—is like walking around with a nerve block. Feels great, even with shards of tibia breaking through the skin, but when the local anesthetic wears off, the pain will be much worse.

The first lesson in this process is empathy. A family didn't want to leave their frail grandmother's side when I was a new nurse, so I enlisted their help to place a nasogastric tube. It wasn't my intention (I was just being my usual practical self), but we quickly aborted the procedure and began a discussion about DNR status. They saw what "do everything you can for her" looked like, and they had empathy. A good practitioner experiences it when starting an IV or inhalational induction on a young child. In the grandmother's case, empathy reveals, "This isn't worth it," while in the child's, the discomfort is necessary for a good outcome. We must be strong enough to truly see their perspective and feel what someone else wants, and still do the right thing. This is much harder than demonizing and opposing the other person. It brings our own hidden motivations to light. We want to deny our shortcomings rather than admit incompetence, but we can't increase anything in life without decreasing something else. Want to be a better father? Your employer will suffer for it. Have the decency not to deceive yourself. Make decisions with clarity and wisdom, even if you find yourself in unexpected circumstances. "I left because I am selfish and my personal values couldn't make me stay and endure." Better than wishing and praying away all but the noblest of motives and behaviors, right? I'm not lecturing anyone—this is a judgment free zone, but I won't prolong your healing with the lidocaine of good intentions and hollow platitudes.

In case you've taken offense in my attempt to make us all better people, not just competent clinicians, let me complete this concept before you tune me out or ask, as I often enjoy doing, "Can someone turn the awkward dial down for me?" Helen Hunt with smoky periwinkle eye shadow in the '90's—no, I'm close, but that's not it—think rather of a certain Disney ice princess singing out, "Let it go!" I propose a new mantra: "Make it right!" This is especially for the spiritual ones among us who may be inclined to release wrongdoing to the universe or pray for forgiveness. Listen, if you have a job and still owe me $100, Jesus might forgive you, but I sure won't until I get my money back. More on forgiveness later.

Sometimes these situations are completely out of our hands, and the best we can do is heal quickly but thoroughly before heading off in a different direction. The decision arcs back to the first section of this chapter and knowing yourself well enough to discern whether a choice exists and you should attempt to fix things. No, they probably aren't worth it, but you're really not doing this for them. My personal challenge is to become unoffendable, but not strive (ie, stretch to depletion) out of legalistic duty to always be the "good guy" during conflict. Let's be honest, people are easy to use if they can't stomach the idea of disappointing others. The concept here is the opposite of what I just preached, but equally valid: hold everything loosely.

The fear of losing what you have approaches life and loved ones from a place of scarcity instead of abundance. Gratitude fades. Why not fiercely grip what's valuable with both hands? How could I hold anesthesia loosely, when I've written books and countless articles about it, worked nonstop from 2000 to 2010 to become a nurse anesthetist, and don't intend to retire or even slow down to 40 hours a week until I have to? I love it! Well, when I close my fist in fear around something, I can't even tell if it is still there. With a gentler grip, I can peer between my fingers and see how it's doing. Literally, fear of failure will make you shaky as you intubate, not to mention the tightening of your fist around a laryngoscope handle will probably impair your angle and any hope of finesse. The finesse of living life with this duality of "make it right" and "hold it loosely" allows for imperfection and grace without selfishness or condemnation. Perhaps more importantly, it prevents the stagnation of gripping something that isn't even there anymore.

When we lose sight of what we have, our own memories start shimmering like a mirage. I journal to keep perspective of both happier and sadder times. Giving of yourself to others is impossible unless you are whole, which is why, if done right, self-care is remarkably unselfish. Track your progress. Sometimes, the emotions stay but the details seep away like ink dampened by the incessant tears of a lonely teenager writing in her diary. A common thread is questioning if it was all a lie and was I ever really happy? That's like asking which memory stream would your mind choose if you built a time machine and changed your past. Don't overcompensate with unrelated matters to make up for unanswerable questions or your own shortcomings. It is what it is. Let's go back 2,000 years with that time machine you just built. No one gives the Jewish priests street cred for using Judas's blood money to bury the homeless. That was so nice of them, but no one cares because of that other thing they did a few days before Easter with the help of the Romans.

Writing down thoughts to remember the beauty of autumn leaves dripping with dew is a much fuller way to live life than attempting to chronicle grudges accurately. Once again we run into the balancing act of forgiving easily while perceiving instances when we are wronged and need to stand up for ourselves. For both the easy-going and the type of people who ruminate endlessly over relatively forgettable circumstances, eventually unforgiveness or living life nonchalantly and burying pain leads to bitterness. In the CRNAs and SRNAs Facebook group, a member casually asked how easy it was to skip out of an education session early at a conference. One person answered his question, but forty outraged CRNAs were offended that he would even consider such grave dishonesty. They questioned his clinical skills and character—only a reprobate wouldn't want to expand their mind with more anesthesia knowledge! I almost commented, "Give me $50 and I'll sign you in," but decided not to feed the monster of offense. Maybe I'm the only one who bases my continuing education on the two factors of 1) what will take the least amount of time and 2) what will take the least amount of money. Every year I write a handful or two of peer reviewed continuation education articles, but it's completely up to the reader to decide whether to apply them and learn.

I keep on coming back to the foolishness of living an offended life full of grudges, because it's central to cutting your losses. I've met so many people who moved on from hurt or relationships prematurely, but still carry wounds in their soul. Isn't that the worst of both worlds? They are the only ones locked in prison. Fear of letting someone "off the hook" prevents both reconciliation and a clean break. Forgiveness is about freeing yourself, while reconciliation is a much riskier endeavor that trusts them not to hurt you again. There is a "dirty grief" associated with preventable loss, to refer back to my analogy of having the money you owe someone but spending it frivolously. In such cases, forgiveness is like a boxing match with shifting momentum and rounds won and lost, especially when the wrong is complex and layered. Grief and despair often come in waves, and especially if you're cutting your losses as we'll discuss later, good days are often followed by bad days. The free app "Calm Harm" provides innovative ways to distract or think better about yourself during moments that tempt you to hurt yourself.

In the case of divorce, it's rarely ever completely one person's fault, although many affairs have to do with opportunity, not the common misconception of someone unable to keep their man or woman. For those who feel used and discarded, they didn't use you because you were weak, but because you had so much to give. Sometimes you end up giving parts of you that really aren't for anyone else—little pieces of your soul—instead of the transparency and openness they really need from you. Of course, if they are acting selfishly, they certainly haven't earned the right to see your most vulnerable side, so it can be an ugly cycle.

It's getting deep and uncomfortable here, but let's push past the abstract and keep it real for just a little longer. How can you become a competent practitioner while barely holding on to a failing relationship? It's better that one succeed rather than both ending in misery, and better to ditch it during the first semester of school or third year of marriage than wasting time fruitlessly. The time invested in both a career and a relationship factors into the equation. Of course, I did mention research that unhappy marriages often get better on their own, and that predicting how someone else will act while under the influence of intense emotions resembles trying to light just one tree on fire in a forest.

In the "Crash and Burn" chapter, I wrote that I had to quit my first attempt at anesthesia school. It wasn't relevant five years ago when I wrote the first edition of this book, but there's another side to that story, one I've never told before. This section is reminding some readers of deep wounds, hurts that may have scabbed over but not completely healed. In exposing such vulnerability, I need to be vulnerable myself. It wasn't a completely conscious decision, but I chose between the girl I was dating at the time and my aspirations to be a nurse anesthetist. I couldn't do both well. I can even pinpoint a fateful clinical day when I wasn't prepared because I put her first. It would have been idiotic to tell her that, of course, and it certainly derailed my plans. It comes back to the fact that you can't do everything and be everything. Some dreams have to die. In the case of marriage, a vow isn't going to be easy to fulfill if you have to do it in a church in front of God and all your friends and get a license from the government.

Practically, for those of you trying to cling to or escape from a relationship while also perfecting the art of anesthesia, I recommend a "no contact" period. You don't have to give a speech beforehand or stop paying child support. It's a drastic move that works best if you have broken up and live apart, without any signs of progress from working things out together or with a counselor. Otherwise, it's a misapplication of boundaries as the weapon of "the silent treatment." Why not vent all your feelings together instead? Well, I'm typing this at a Starbucks in the hippest part of Cleveland (it's not Detroit—such places exist). The woman next to me can't get her iPhone to work right, so she's beating it. Literally slapping it around. Everyone else in this crowded coffee shop is noticeably perturbed that they must share this establishment with the village idiot. I, of course, have a wide grin on my face and am trying my best not to chortle into my child's size hot chocolate. Hurting people hurt people, and as Francis Frangipane says, criticism makes us defensive instead of "at home" with another person's soul. Attempts to ignore offense, to say the right thing when a relationship is already gone, work as well as articulating the coagulation cascade to a student as we run away from a bear. With trust gone, words lose their power. How both people make each other feel about the relationship, and more than that, consistent actions are what matters.

Either disregarding or obeying feelings is like symptom management that, ten prescriptions later, never gets to the core problem. For example, in some circles of functional medicine, crippling anxiety or depression isn't treated with the Prozac-like qualities of St. John's Wort. Rather, hair mineral analysis testing for unbound copper pinpoints the right dose of zinc picolinate and whether oral chelation is an option to permanently change

91

biochemistry. Feelings are simply clues to what lies under the surface, which is why an "emotional fast" from the other person is both illuminating and dangerous. Hunger for emotional connection is similar to the effects of fasting food, which itself is a useful spiritual discipline for self examination. When we are depleted, we zero in on crumbs of affection or appreciation from any available source as if they were chocolate cake, even if we're normally gluten free.

To lessen that ravenous emotional hunger, try to establish at least a minimal emotional connection with your loved one before contacting them only when absolutely necessary. Otherwise, all you might feel is relief that they are no longer stressing you out. The purpose of this whole exercise is to reset and avoid making complex life decisions from your panicking reflex-driven amygdala. Many experts recommend a month. This is 100% my idea, but the length of a no contact period should correlate with your success in school. Did your husband have an affair right before your last semester? Tell him you won't be having any linen closet/chocolate cake adventures, but not to bother calling you until after you pass boards. If he's only remorseful about being caught, he'll be gone by then, but if he's willing to explore unresolved issues from childhood and do the work needed to become a more trustworthy person, you can have your chocolate cake and eat it too. I really need to stop fasting meals before writing.

"Set it in place and call for movement." That saying from Dr. Rolf is about lining up muscle fascia and developing good posture habits, but it's an analogy for creating good habits and walking them out. Relationship wisdom does nothing for you unless implemented. A no contact period will destroy any hope of having the same relationship with your spouse or loved one, but it does allow you to move on—hopefully with the same person, but in a more functional relationship. Instead of trying to intubate roughly over and over with a Mac 3, it's pausing and calling for the Glidescope. The emphasis is still on empathy and doing the right thing. Sometimes the right thing doesn't look like the best option or most fulfilling alternative, especially in the short term. Caring for yourself isn't simply indulgence in the form of bonbons and bath bombs. Sometimes it's self-care in the form of sacrificing happiness for others. Coming through on commitments, choosing the difficult path, and offering grace and forgiveness to those trying to change can nourish the soul more than mud baths and massages ever could. Fill yourself with occasional moments of exquisite bliss as a safeguard from depletion. That's why I adapted this topic specifically for nurse anesthetists. We give of ourselves every day at work. Our closest relationships require a different kind of outpouring than the caregiver's swirl of effort, kindness, smiling through clenched teeth instead of rolling our eyes, and bonding with others by complaining.

Resources

Although typically referring to engines, RPM could also stand for Results, Purpose, Method. Before I can actualize the results I want, I need to choose the right method and line that up with a reason why I've chosen a particular goal. I've spoken to many authors of relationship books to glean from their individual insights, and I've adapted RPM from Brian Mulipah. If you are in an abusive relationship with an unrepentant jerk, the desired result is to get out as safely, cleanly, and quickly as possible. I'll discuss counseling to discern the right method and purpose for a change in your relationships, but RPM is a useful tool to filter out unhelpful voices and focus on what needs to happen now and in the future. It's best to make decisions before the compelling opportunity to make a stupid choice presents itself.

We're about to leave relationships and talk about finances in the next chapter, so let's get a head start and talk about affordable counseling. Many churches and universities offer free counseling, although quality and availability differ widely. Employee wellness is also an option if you're desperate enough. I hesitate because any one of the websites or newsletters I'll soon mention is infinitely better than incompetent guidance. Training and experience is critical, but it's not the most important thing. Similar to seeing a chiropractor, positive recommendations from those who've been there and still walk straight is invaluable. As elected officials prove to us continually, just because someone shares the same important beliefs doesn't mean they are wise and give relevant advice. Nor should you choose a therapist because they'll go easy on your issue or are especially against whatever problems your partner has. There is obviously less freedom in saying exactly what's on your mind in couples counseling, while the disadvantage of individual counseling is that the counselor only has access to your perspective.

Some evidence argues that counseling doesn't improve relationships or decrease divorce rates. Especially if you are unsure of a counselor's expertise, doing more of the talking to make sense of your own thoughts and decision process may be better initially than seeking exact guidance. I personally prefer someone who leads me into the right thing rather than fostering the realization of what I really want and pursuing that. Either way, choose actions that grow you into becoming better—the result will impact your clinical decisions too. An arterial line is superior to a blood pressure cuff, but it's a clear case of the best option not being the right option—are you really going to place one for each endoscopy?

Counseling is not a magic bullet any more than adding ketamine to midazolam and fentanyl when sedating the endoscopy patient we almost stabbed in the wrist last sentence because "safety first." Sometimes, that drug combination far surpasses aggressively giving propofol and having to accept oxygen saturations and blood pressures slightly lower than normal. On rare occasions, patients have laryngospams from the ketamine, forget to breathe because of the fentanyl, or wake up slowly because of the midazolam. In the end, it's timing and doing the necessary work that matters, not just having the right tools. You can finish this book and several more, but unless you apply the right principles, it won't matter.

Several steps removed from PhD, CSW, MFT, MHC, and other acronyms for counselors are life coaches (recall my snide comments about four week Internet courses and pretty social media pictures). I haven't recommended any specific counselors, but I've always been impressed with Presence Coaching. Much of their work happens in small group conference calls rather than costly weekends at group intensives. The small and doable beats an expensive memory, although sometimes a couple does need to get away from other influences to hash things out. Survey multiple influences to find sustainable inspiration as you grow individually and with others. Ooh, that was a $10 sentence in a $7 book. Sure sounds fancy and like I should have edited it out. Some of you bought this book because of my diversity initiatives or articles written for "Minority Nurse." *The Blueprint* by Kirk Franklin and *Lies at the Altar* by Robin L Smith are both excellent if the confines of the white and suburban pop culture approach to relationships need not apply.

The next two websites are in line with the philosophies of Gary Thomas, Chapman, and Smalley about working life out with someone who, like you, is less than ideal. They come from a Christian perspective instead of one consistently putting your own needs first. "Consistently" is the key word. Eventually, no one is of use at work or home if they don't take care of their own emotional well-being. Ultimatehusband.com contains unique insights, such as, "The number one lie in marital conflict is, 'This separation will be only temporary.'" The site offers new perspectives on male defensiveness from misinterpreting his partner's fear as she loses trust. Trying to control everything once her husband loses her trust is a main cause of wife- instigated divorce, unlike husbands, who often divorce after a promotion. Marriage Builders contains all sorts of practical ideas, including how to structure work relationships, and I'm sure some of them will resonate as doable in your particular situation.

For an approach opposite that of a devoted, sacrificial person of faith, fxckfeelings.com is an insightful and hilarious resource for assessing life as it is. Latching onto a higher power for the sole purpose of reducing situational pain has drawbacks, after all. On his clever website, Dr. Lastname favors an analytical approach rather than trusting the gut, groin, or heart. Shedding the complexities of life to see the naked, ugly truth allows you to move past perceptions and see reality as you make decisions. Years of suppressing emotions (and it's not just health care: anyone in retail, customer service, etc. can relate) leads to the inability to just let feelings be. A metal detector isn't the same as an X-Ray. In all of their ferocity, emotions guide us to follow them and expose hidden fears and desires. Don't make decisions based on emotions or censor them from your intellect. That's a difficult balance when *Talking to Crazy*, a book by Mark Goulston. Not that probiotics will heal your marriage, but poorly understood health issues contained outside the brain devastate relationships, as if the only choices are "diagnosable mental illness" or "crabby person." I know people who divorced because that was safer for them then coming to terms with unacceptable thoughts like, "If my wife and kid just vanished tomorrow, anesthesia school would be so much easier." It can be so healing to tell someone, "I know this is hard, and you've probably thought ___. That doesn't make you a bad person; it's like writing down random thoughts in a journal to unscramble your brain." Goulston's take-away point is that there are many ways, from confrontation to compliments, to get through to the people who create the most drama in our lives.

For those without that special someone right now, sign up for Dr. Randi Gunther's newsletter, which tackles relationship and dating issues with profound clarity. During my research, I kept seeing ads for "Getting your Ex Back," and each self-styled guru was worse and more expensive than the last. But, it's not like I have any acronyms following my name associated with counseling expertise either, so I do recommend two of them. The first is Clay Andrew's, because he focuses on authenticity rather than the right words to say. All the right moves and expert coaching are inferior to a man or woman with integrity and authenticity. The willingness to be rejected for who you truly are, as painful as that may be, rather than play games and shield your true self and vulnerabilities—that's compelling right there. It shows leadership, which husbandhelphaven.com describes as the essence of what every woman craves, whether she is with an alpha male or a passive nice guy. Stephen Waldo's resources explain what it means to be a real man, as opposed to a blustering and controlling or weak and submissive caricature trying to keep his relationship together.

Time to summarize the last 12,500 words in a witty paragraph! Just like star athletes/members of the Cleveland Browns simultaneously exhibit great skill and terrible life decisions, our emotional and spiritual intelligence must keep up with our expertise. When it doesn't, relationships die, clinicians die (from fentanyl abuse), and we are all poorer because of it. "Fake it 'til you make it" and shallow encouragement as we sprint through life leaves us with meaningless trophies. Concentrate on what matters. Love on those who matter most in your life. There is always a deeper level of intimacy and understanding, but it takes a team effort to get there. Your name isn't followed by RN or PA because you did your share and gave 50%. Be all in: 100%, and don't be afraid to acknowledge when you feel overwhelmed. Physician, you don't have to heal all by yourself any longer. After walking through the grief, the new you will be stronger and wiser, and we can't wait to get to know them.

Finances

Soul Spending & Saving

Let me begin with a clever segue between romance and money so I won't have to add a new chapter picture with the words "Chapter $." As with relationships, I'm trying to avoid a tone suggesting that you are messed up. Despite my articles, interviews, and speaking engagements about all of the topics in this book, my expertise is more in learning from asinine mistakes and explaining dry, complex themes in entertaining and actionable ways than anything else. I don't want to occasionally throw in a "we" to feign humility among my abundant use of the pronoun "you." This whole book could be filled with mistakes "I" have made, but talking about myself is only a surreptitious reason this work exists, not the primary driver. I haven't talked extensively about emotional scars, but they wreck financial goals just like they do relationships. Recognize and deal with scars so they exist only as a lesson and a story. Otherwise, scars remain chronic wounds, the pain temporarily assuaged by someone with similar wounds or an unwise purchase. That purchase could be a purse, sports car, or just a hoarder lifestyle.

First paragraph, and I'm already throwing around great words like "emotional scars" and "assuaged." They won't stay with you once you go do something else, but perhaps a personal example will. I'm circling back to control issues toward yourself and others, like the poor analogy earlier about sedating a patient on the edge of a knife with four different drugs exhibiting various onset, duration, and potency, as opposed to one imperfect but reliable drug. One of my emotional scars is from a subconscious vow I made as I exited my teenage years. Subconscious vows become scripts we follow and patterns of behavior based on life-shaping events. Rigid rules set during unrelated circumstances decrease flexibility to solve life's problems. It may not have been a conscious decision to never drink alcohol like Dad did or to smoke two packs a day just like Mom. Is your internal rulebook valid and helpful?

A common subconscious vow for high achievers is, "As long as I'm successful, they'll love me." In my situation, I grappled with how to treat a close female friend once she obtained a boyfriend. I didn't know the meaning of "ambivalence" back then and felt torn about the right way forward. I'd already performed the noble act of fading into the background several times as a friendly, disarming, but romantically unambitious teenager, and I was tired of it. The drama resolved with her quoting, "Friendship includes, but love excludes." Many years later, I realized that, since that moment, I'd shaped much of my life around that phrase by trying to live the opposite. At the cost of personal boundaries, I'd let people in while not prioritizing relationships correctly, which was just as wrong as that weird couple who think "guys night" or "girls night" is the first slippery step towards divorce.

The thought might cross your mind, "Cute awkward story, Bruh, but what does that have to do with making me a Bitcoin millionaire?" Our saving and spending habits come from unexplored places in the soul that stall efforts to live a life without fear or, in the case of free-spirited spenders, plan effectively for the future. A key takeaway from last chapter is that will power can't build a lasting, fulfilling relationship any more than it will transform you into an excellent clinician. Determination is crucial, but not the answer. An anesthesia provider returning from rehab has more resolve than anyone else in the hospital to never feel that buzz from intravenous fentanyl, but some clinicians have to give up clinical practice forever. I'm not saying that someone starting a diet should become a chocolatier to reveal their weaknesses, but that all of us have finite reserves of self control. I didn't always believe this—as a nurse I purposely chose a patient for thirteen days in a row who had sent every other nurse out of his room screaming at him or crying. By day ten we became buddies, although I drew the line at day fourteen. But, life is unexpected and inexorable, and anything exhaustible can be depleted. I could continue with a caveat about spirituality and the concept of abundance and an overflowing cup, but in the case of finances, an early start makes an incredible difference. Also, it will allow you to ignore the riskier investments I'll discuss at length later (simply because information on safer strategies is readily available).

Our personal traumatic or pleasant life experiences shape our thoughts on money, comfort, and security. Media and culture interact to shift priorities. I disagree with the portrayal of Greece as a lazy, debt-ridden country, but it's true that for many Greeks, financial aspirations beyond a stable government pension stop at having enough money for coffee and spanakopita with friends at a café. I will take that any day over the American mindset of making just a little more money in case the 401K doesn't work out. If the stock market were to bottom out, your original $3,000,000 or $2,000,000 saved up wouldn't look all that different.

Advertisements prey on our fears and insecurities. Notice the indirect way that a pimple cream or razor ad infers how unwanted you will be without smooth, flawless skin. About 100 years ago, Gillette realized they could double sales if women would start shaving body hair. If a company can't get you to buy their product because you feel bad about yourself, they'll resort to "you deserve this." On rare occasions in a relationship, saying that you feel you deserve something can express clear expectations and foster honest communication, but we've seen nagging thoughts of discontentment and disappointment poison even the best things in life. It's not difficult to make money in the stock market betting against people trying to hit a home run every time instead of settling for safe, reliable gains. "Safe and reliable" may be a misnomer as the connections among companies, economic sectors, and countries increase in complexity and opaqueness.

Before the Great Recession, people spent more money because rising real estate prices provided security, and no one was inventing more land to drive down home prices. Ten years later, businesses are still hoarding money rather than spending it on research or increasing wages. Money in checking accounts and certificates of deposit loses value compared to inflation, and most Americans are still living paycheck to paycheck. We don't want our assets stolen from us and hesitate to grow investments until everyone else jumps in and the easy money is gone. That doesn't sound comfortable, and yet making our lives comfortable is the lure of many purchases. That's not to say you should be a miser as I am, questioning the ultimate worth of every single purchase. Buying a cheap office chair will cost you more in replacements and chiropractor bills. High quality items are often worth the extra cost. Thankfully I learned this as a child, though not until my fourth $10 video game joystick broke during a barrel roll. I almost lost our nation to the Communists and their MiG fighters because of that.

Time should be the ultimate deciding factor for expenditures, not comfort, security, prestige, fear, or generosity. I don't give a dollar to the person in front of me in the grocery store to pay it forward. You can't make more time, and I don't want to lose five minutes of it permanently while she digs around her change purse or tries to write a check. Saving time allows the cultivation of deep, intimate relationships on a daily basis. Rather than running the rat race in between expensive vacations, use money to free up time and live life fully, using the principles we learned last chapter, of course. I'm not suggesting a live-in nanny, paying someone to mow your lawn every week, or one of those services where the dirty laundry gets trucked away and returned cleaned and neatly folded. But, occasionally hiring someone to do a lengthy task, like cleaning your house before the holidays, prevents stress and bottlenecks that eat up valuable time. This same principle is why working overtime when an employer is desperate one week and leaving early every day the next makes more money than equally spacing eighty hours of work every two weeks. Such nimbleness requires a "time budget" to ensure taking care of yourself and loved ones takes priority over less important but more urgent tasks, such as a mountain of dirty dishes.

Budgeting is a useful method to prioritize time over money, unless that activity takes considerable time and effort just to discover why last month's financial goals went off the rails. I'm pretty sure we can all agree that the cause was spending more and saving less than the budget called for. Grow wealth by working for overtime or extra incentives, but since the time to do so is limited, passive income—the ability to make money while you sleep, eat, and do everything besides work—should be a part of everyone's empire building strategy. This isn't limited to physicians with their ability to invest large amounts and buy franchises or businesses for other people to manage. It's harder and not as much fun to invest in something you don't understand and lack interest in. Springboard existing hobbies into sources of income, but remember that time is the ultimate currency. Ten years ago, putting up an online store or publishing a book could yield a trickle of sustainable income. Today you can repeatedly beg a thousand Facebook friends to buy into your pyramid scheme, and they'll still avoid you in person, lest any conversation suddenly take a vicious turn to weight-shedding magic shakes. Before we venture any farther, I offer my peer-reviewed overview into relevant financial topics for nurses. Please read before the temptation to buy into an ill-advised opportunity to lose all your friends takes root.

Managing Finances

After reading this article, the learner should be able to:
1. Discuss novel methods to maximize returns on investments while focusing on present needs.
2. Learn to maximize employee benefits to save money for school, retirement, healthcare, and other needs.
3. Plan wisely for disability, retirement, and death.

How do most nurses respond when they shake the piggy bank and find it empty? Do they budget and quit visiting the overpriced and underdelicious hospital cafeteria? Do they start nursing blogs hoping to make millions from their ramblings about last week's three to eleven shifts on the colorectal floor? Or maybe they reduce debt by resisting a new purchase and driving a paid-off car too beaten up to ever sneak into the physician's parking lot. Actually, because the majority of them are paid hourly, they simply work more.[1] Night shifts, weekend shifts and extra overtime provide a fatter paycheck, but without proper planning, nurses may soon find themselves endangering their nursing license and their health, not to mention patient safety. The author once fell asleep and totaled his car after an extra night shift. Once his car came to an abrupt stop inside the car in front of him, he continued his nap after verifying no one was seriously injured.

Average Yearly Salaries

Before discussing finances any further, it is important to discuss demographics. Statistics will not be discussed in detail as they speak for themselves about the factors leading to higher income. Defining average compensation accurately can be difficult; nurses work in a variety of settings with completely different roles and pay scales, so for the sake of equal comparisons, salary information is from the *2015 Association of periOperative Registered Nurses Salary and Compensation Survey.* The majority of respondents were between forty and fifty-nine years old, held a bachelor's degree in nursing, and worked at acute care hospitals. The average staff nurse earns $68,600 yearly, continuing a slight upswing since 2013. Directors of nursing spend 19% of their time on direct patient care, as opposed to 90% for staff nurses, and average an income of $112,800 yearly. Office-based staff nurses earn $10,600 less than average, and nurses working in free-standing surgical centers receive $4,500 less. In 2015, nurses in specialty hospitals make $2,700 more and those in academic medical centers $1,300 more than nurses in general and community hospitals. Smaller hospitals pay less and government/federal hospitals pay $7,000 more than average. [1]

In order, nurses receive more money in the Pacific region, followed by Mid-Atlantic and New England. Nurses in Massachusetts receive an average $27,600 more than the New England average, and those in Tennessee, Iowa, and Pennsylvania make roughly $7,000 less than expected. Those in rural areas also receive reduced compensation. Salaried nurses earn more than hourly workers by almost $2,000 yearly, although separate statistics show that they work the most overtime. Increased experience leads to substantially higher pay only in the first few years of a nurse's career. Additional certifications do not contribute significantly to compensation, although a master's degree does add an additional $4,100, adjusted for specific job titles. Although union affiliation increases pay, family and gender roles for the average nurse have affected pay differently each year of the survey. This year, women with children in the home earned $900 less than average. [1]

Knowledge Gap

To confirm the idea that many nurses plan to work longer as their primary financial solution, researchers asked nurses about the importance of financial planning. They discovered that all nurses need to focus on financial preparation and begin the process at the beginning of their careers. Only 24% had planned a strategy, although 71% of those surveyed intended to retire by age 60. The top four strategies involved physical and mental healthiness rather than financial planning. Pensions and savings were the two vehicles intended to fund the nurses in their later years. However, the nurses were unsure how much money they needed to save. [2] In other words, many nurses intend to ensure financial security by being healthy enough to lift patients and resist emotional burnout indefinitely.

The literature on nurses and their money is quite limited, but raises concern about limited planning and possible reasons for this. Career breaks for children, starting nursing school at a later age, and part-time or contract positions all relate to the lack of cohesive planning. The fact that nursing is still a female-dominated profession with a history of low wages is relevant, and being financially illiterate or thinking financial planning should be more a man's role are other possibilities. [2,3] To fill educational gaps, potential workshops should include retirement and benefits, budgeting and investments decisions, life and disability insurance, and taxes and legal issues. Financial planning does not exist in a vacuum and should also entail the psychosocial components of role and career transitions, time management and work alternatives, and physical components of fitness, nutrition, stress management, and health care needs. [2]

Short Term Investments

Many financial advisors place emergency savings as the top priority when discussing a financial plan. Keeping the equivalent of a quarter to half a year's salary in liquid (easily accessible and can be quickly turned into cash) assets seemed more logical when savings accounts and certificates of deposit gained 3% yearly. [4] Any discussions about interest rates and related investments or loans are time sensitive and may not be as relevant several years after this article is published. For example, when originally formulating this article in the last quarter of 2015, the author intended to suggest that readers invest in physical bars of precious metals such as gold, palladium, and platinum, using websites such as comparesilverprices.com. When he sat down to begin writing this paper in the first quarter of 2016, his alternative to savings accounts was to build a ladder of high yield bonds that would return money invested plus interest at regular intervals, similar to opening certificate of deposit accounts of varying lengths so that money would be available every six months or so. [4] Neither of those ideas are terrible today, but the time to lock in impressive profits by choosing one of those undervalued investments has probably passed.

An emergency fund is essentially part of risk management— preparing for the unexpected. The unexpected is influenced by current debts, children, health status, and basically anything for which a nurse may require insurance. Specifics on insurance needs will be discussed later. Besides sustaining a nurse between jobs, emergency funds provide a buffer for home and auto repairs, medical emergencies, and other events that could otherwise seriously thwart financial planning. [5] One method is to set aside $20 to $100 dollars a month into an account that is off limits. The goal is to avoid using credit cards during emergencies and starting the ugly and expensive cycle of debt. [4]

As stated above, this money should be fairly liquid, but portions of it do not need to be locked in a bank or stuffed under a mattress for immediate access. While certificates of deposit let the bank borrow a nurse's money, bonds allow companies or government entities to borrow money from the public and return it with interest at a specified time. They are safer than stock from the same company, although they are not guaranteed. The advantage of municipal bonds is that they can be bought outside of a tax sheltered account—such as a Roth Individual Retirement Account (IRA)—and still not have taxes due on the interest. With the exception of high yield (essentially meaning higher risk of bankruptcy) bonds mentioned previously, interest rates are lower for the short borrowing times required to use this approach to save for school and similarly timed needs. [4]

Alternative Investments

Much like a nurse shouldn't give the patient in 403B twenty units of insulin because it worked so well for the patient in 403A, much of the information in this article is highly individualized. This is especially true for the controversial topic of alternative investments, which are basically the opposite of the safe and serene mutual funds typical of employer sponsored retirement plans, or even the index funds best suited to simplify individual investment with minimal fees. The concept is higher risk with higher rewards while investing in products not highly correlated with the stock market and retirement accounts that depend on it. Risk is best described as how quickly and often an asset changes value in relation to other investments. [5] Alternative investments may seem to be beyond the scope of this article, as they are defined as complex investments that because of their complicated nature or structure, are not generally suitable to the public, but this is an ignored topic that can help nurses diversify their investments. Physical products such as precious metals, art, wine, or cars are examples. Perhaps selling a Beanie Babies collection over the Internet doesn't sound as sophisticated as storing gold bullion in a safe, but the key word is "alternative." Peer-to-peer lending (ie between people without banks) or tax liens are also viable strategies that allow the nurse to operate as a bank to loan (or borrow) money with much higher interest rates than savings or money market accounts. However, more traditional choices are hedge funds, certain types of stock trades, and investments into private companies. Many of these financial instruments are much less regulated than the stock market and require more in-depth research. [6]

Investing in private companies used to be a practice reserved for accredited investors with incomes much higher than the average nurse salaries quoted earlier. This is because some private companies multiply investments at rates much higher than the stock market, but many lose every cent. However, recent passage of Title III and Title IV of the JOBS Act has allowed companies to use crowdfunding from just about anyone in return for shares of their company. Participation requires signing up on a website "portal" that offers access to companies accepting investments. Nurses investing a few hundred or thousand dollars into these companies can expect regular dividends if the company buys real estate. Most other companies must be viewed as medium to long term investments, as investors are unlikely to get their money back until the company joins the public stock market or has a similar liquidity event. Unfortunately, often that event is bankruptcy resulting in a total loss. While nurses may lack the sophistication of venture capitalists to pick winning companies, the fact that some of these startups are healthcare related does allow nurses to invest in what they know. [7]

Clearly, nurses should only throw money they can afford to lose into alternative investments, but the same can be said for lottery tickets or betting on a lousy nurse manager's firing date. Perhaps with the exception of real estate or peer-to-peer lending, the conservative investments of a nurse ready to retire have no use for alternative investments. Generally, one type of alternative investment should not exceed 15% of a portfolio, and many experts suggest only 5% of retirement savings should be in alternative investments. Also, many financial companies allow fund managers to explore these sorts of investments worldwide within a mutual fund structure. Scams are still common that sound "too good to be true", but the key reason to invest alternatively is diversification, so that different types of savings aren't all increasing or decreasing in value at the same time. [6]

Financial advisors often talk about investing into products that will gain more value in the future or provide growth. Alternative investing is a part of the value versus growth debate. It seeks to invest in fledgling companies or products, but the industry is poised to grow quickly and provide the type of data and standardization more recognizable in today's stock market. A key goal in any kind of investing is discovering "what's hot" before everyone else does, rather than piling in once most of the money is already made. By 2020, today's alternative investing will more resemble "active asset management" or "multi-asset class solutions." Especially in the developing nations that comprise riskier portions of the stock market, increased building, buying, and borrowing will inject more money into alternative investments. [8]

Budgets

Alternative investments are unwise without a working budget in place to explain the cost of a lousy investment or the benefit of a profitable one to a nurse's financial picture. Wise financial decisions come from risk tolerance, and that's difficult to perceive without understanding the flow of money from paycheck to savings to spending. Of course, "budget" is a word filled with negative imagery, analogous to "mandatory overtime" or "fecal impaction." Begin by tracking spending for a month and differentiating needs from wants. For example, resisting the urge to buy a daily latte saves more than $1,000 yearly. Separating saved money before bills are paid and resisting the urge to spend money from raises and bonuses also makes budgeting easier, as opposed to simply doing math to highlight poor financial decisions after the fact, month after month. Sustainable discipline, starting with small, discretionary purchases, allows the nurse to develop a plan to move more unassigned dollars into savings. A yearly self-audit is also helpful to gauge progress and make sure that saved money is being invested appropriately. [9]

Benefits

Although they are rarely taken into consideration, retention pay, the incredible tax advantages of health saving accounts (HSAs), education days, and the exact structure of more traditional benefits all factor into budgeting and finances, especially as more obscure benefits are actually declining. Even if it requires a boring meeting in the Human Resource department, familiarity with pay structure also assists planning. Understanding the details of overtime and off shift pay differentials and even employee discounts helps the nurse work smarter, not harder. Shift differentials for working at night averages 10% of hourly pay. Being on-call garners nurses $3.50 an hour, with only 60% of respondents automatically receiving time-and-a-half pay if called in. Although hourly nurses are well aware that working thirty hours one week and fifty the next results in a bigger than working forty hours both weeks, budgeting time and energy is just as important as budgeting money. [1]

Because of rising tuition costs and the crippling effect of too much debt, tuition reimbursement is an important benefit for nurses to understand. Time, cost, and effort are all hindrances to obtaining more education, as is the lack of organized career ladders that encourage nurses to stay at their institution and progress academically. Recall that pay doesn't increase substantially with more education unless the initials following a nurse's name also change. As with enrolling into retirement plans, early planning to meet the requirements and receive the most money is paramount. Student loans also require scrutiny and occasionally an expert opinion to make sure that extra schooling more than pays for education debts. The glorious math of compound interest that accelerates savings placed into high interest accounts can also increase debt in certain types of loans. [1, 10]

Most benefit packages include disability and life insurance. Although their purpose is much different than alternative investments, the concept of highly individualized differences still applies. Will planning is also an inexpensive but critical part of this process. Especially for primary breadwinners, supplemental policies offer methods to ensure household financial stability if tragedy occurs. Riders exist to allow life insurance money to pay for longer term care and other needs that would otherwise need a different policy. Permanent life insurance exists until the policy holder dies. Term insurance is cheaper and serves to provide protection for a specific, usually critical, period of time. Various types of life insurance instruments also function as investments. Their main advantages often appeal to those in higher income brackets requiring more vehicles to grow income without additional taxes. As with all the topics discussed in this article, insight from a trusted financial advisor helps illuminate specific needs for each situation, but it is useful to know whether an expert is paid from selling insurance products or by a set amount of fees. [1,5]

Retirement

If nurses need trusted experts to guide insurance, investment, and retirement planning, what is the purpose of financial education? The nursing processes of assessment, diagnosis, planning, implementation, and evaluation assist the nurse to make sound financial decisions. Nursing skills lend themselves to wise delegation on topics better suited for financial advisors.[4] Retirement planning is the only topic in this article that is thoroughly studied in the literature, with many nurses feeling inadequate and unprepared, fearing the stock market, and wishing that their employers provided education about financial planning. One reason is the demise of defined-benefit pensions in favor of defined-contribution retirement accounts. Much like social security benefits, the first guarantees a precise, monthly dollar amount in retirement. The latter depends much more on adequate planning and an agreeable stock market. [3, 9]

A 401(k) plan for employees of privately held corporations is the most common example and allows the nurse to defer taxes from investments (most often mutual funds) until they are withdrawn. Employers contribute a percentage to employee's accounts, and that money becomes the nurse's once they are "vested" by working at an institution for several years. Because some plans match contributions the nurse makes, the exact details of how to maximize employer contributions matter greatly so the nurse doesn't pass up free money. Roth versions of these accounts require investments with post-tax dollars, but any money made is not taxed again. For example, a nurse owning stocks providing quarterly dividends in a Roth account would not have to pay taxes on the yield. With certain limitations, employer-provided retirement accounts can also be supplemented with individual retirement accounts. Nurses can contribute more money to these accounts at a certain age, but depending on the type of account may need to withdraw funds as well at a certain age. [3, 9]

Conclusion

By spending time developing a thorough financial plan, nurses can make wiser workplace decisions. Do they really need to sign up for inconvenient overtime shifts or stay at a toxic job with bullying coworkers? Decisions about moving to a nicer house or buying long term care insurance are all much easier with individualized financial goals in place. A mature nurse may not need life insurance and be concerned with preserving her savings rather than multiplying them, while another can afford more aggressive investing once multiple insurance needs are addressed. Peace of mind is priceless, and maximizing employee benefits while saving for the short, medium, and long term is an excellent way to accomplish that.

References

1. Bacon D, Stewart, K. Results of the 2015 AORN salary and compensation survey. *AORN.* 2015;10(8):561-575.
2. Blakely, J., Ribeiro, V. Are nurses prepared for retirement? *J Nurs Manag.* 2008;16:744-752.
3. Keele, S., Alpert, P. Retirement financial planning and the RN. *JONA.* 2013;43(11):574-580.
4. Yarkony, K. Personal finance: There are no shortcuts to financial security. AORN. 2009;90(6):845-850.
5. Cornelison, P. Financial triage. *J Perianesth Nurs.* 1999;14(3):144-149.
6. Halbert, G. Alternative investments: What are they, part I. *Profutures.* 2016. Retrieved from http://profutures.com/article.php/219

Debt

Oh, how you'll miss those cutesy little numbers showing valid sources for everything I write. That's the benefit of writing a $200 article as opposed to a $12 book. We'll return to some of the topics highlighted or provide additional resources at the end of this chapter. I took an informal survey of CRNAs, and the topic that received the most interest was debt. We'll talk about the present debt of student loans, credit cards, and mortgages; preventing the pain of children's student loans in the future; and how to profit off the debt of other people and companies.

Through a lottery system not unlike choosing children to fight to the death in an arena, the government pays some student loans for clinicians in underserved areas. Repayment programs change rapidly, and my focus for this section is to provide awareness readers can follow up with an Internet search. Some companies specialize in refinancing student loans or providing loans to start a new practice. Choosing between paying off a 5% loan or making 5.2% interest off an investment should favor paying off the debt. Emergency savings don't need to have as much money lying around lazily not making more money if debts are minimal. Also, taxes cost time as well as money, especially if you're like me and have all sorts of complex accounts. Don't be scared of low interest loans for your car or home, although they are different as cars depreciate and homes outside of the Rust Belt appreciate. They free up money to pay off credit cards and unsecured loans. Building up your credit score isn't worth it if you continually pay fees and interest charges, so there's also nothing wrong with going "cash only" until gaining control of your finances.

Debt relief agencies are not the way to go. Talking to your lender may work just as well without the extra cost or high interest rates that come with "manageable payments." Lending Club or credit unions may offer better rates than a typical bank to consolidate debt. Lending Club used to be one of my favorite investments, but I think the rise of blockchain technology (decentralized methods to safely store transactions and information) will decrease the interest investors earn from their loans. Similar to staking a poker player, more options exist every day to fund people and businesses with the skill to generate money by opening restaurants, making movies, refinancing church bonds, or trading cryptocurrencies (digital, blockchain powered money not issued by governments). Scams abound, so stick with trusted websites such as wefunder.com for these debt instruments, and read the fine print to see if you're buying debt, equity (stock shares of the company), or some hybrid assurance of payback once a venture is profitable. County tax liens in some states bequeath houses or property at substantial discounts. Although in Florida I can get 18% interest on many loans once the delinquent party pays the lien, I don't invest in them anymore because it takes so much work. I did find it fascinating to log onto the county portal and see who didn't pay their property tax. When searching for the best rates for any payment requiring responsible customers with steady income, see if you qualify for "doctor loans."

For example, USAA qualifies SRNAs for home loans while they're still in graduate school, and my current loans to build a holistic anesthesia and mental health clinic are from companies specializing in funding medical entrepreneurs.

Saving up for a child's college costs is a prudent decision even for a nephew or niece, because of the tax benefits and better looking FAFSA if they apply for financial aid. Simple, conservative investments to select and forget are ideal. Because some benefits in state programs vanish if you move, a 529 plan from a brokerage (if you already use Fidelity, E-Trade, etc.) should include choices available no matter where you live or which state your children attend college. If the plan allows it, a college investment account should include individual bonds that mature the year they graduate high school. For the riskiest part of that portfolio, buy a high yield bond for $800 from a beaten down company unlikely to go bankrupt, and besides the interest payments, you'll earn the extra $200 once it matures. Articles on Seeking Alpha aggregate opinions on a company's future, although instinctively following every analysis is a quick path to financial chaos. Preferred stocks, if picked correctly, provide the growth of stocks and the stable income of bonds, thus diversifying the account beyond mutual funds and ETFs (which are best described as passive, low fee mutual funds tracking a specific index).

Preserving Wealth

I planned to break down investments into safe and risky options, but it makes more sense to consider the overall goal. I am concentrating on crazier options simply because few others have objectively and accurately. Rich people concern themselves with not losing what they have before they can bequeath it to the next generation. That's why the argument fails that highly successful people use a certain investment instrument as a tax shelter and you should too so you can be rich like them. Let's face it: the absurdly wealthy often invest in absurd opportunities because they don't have anywhere else to put their money. Similar to buying eggs from sad, caged chickens, building a vault to bathe in your own money is frowned upon unless you're Scrooge McDuck.

Upon graduation day, as you threw your cap into the air, you may have observed birds circling overhead. Those were actually financial advisors preparing to dive bomb you with expensive universal and whole life insurance policies. Here's the most important statement in this section: preserving wealth is expensive if you don't have any. We insure ourselves to death in case the toaster, cell phone, apartment, wife, or pelvis breaks. Shockingly, the insurance companies often give us less than they should to replace that car, house, or boat. Or hip. That's not to say you should be as fearless as I am, but poverty is more expensive than wealth. You'll need that extended warranty and top-rate insurance if you don't have the funds to deal with the unexpected. That's one of the draws of universal life insurance: you can simplify and take a loan out from the policy to pay for school or emergencies. Although some policies invest in the stock market, the data financial advisors show about life insurance dividends being more reliable than creating wealth from Wall Street is at least partially true. Statistics can be manipulated to show anything. The answer is not to shove a lump sum towards an expensive policy, but to diversify without losing track of all your investments. A whole life policy can also function as a disability policy in some cases. Like time, health is a finite resource of more value than money, so look into some of the resources in the "About the Author" section written to improve your physical and emotional health. CNBC interviewed me about this topic because we don't plan for our future health needs as we do financial needs. The about me section of this book also has links to contact me for more elementary or advanced info on these topics, and a link to the free audio version of *How to Succeed in Anesthesia School.*

Turn off your oxygen tank for a few breaths and look in a mirror. Is your face turning blue? If so, you won't qualify for the same permanent life insurance rates as a perfectly healthy person will, so don't bother with this kind of investment. But, if your husband is quite happy with his job at the car wash, your kids are young, and you're not eligible to invest more in a Roth IRA or other tax shelter, this type of policy may be beneficial if it comes with a financial advisor beyond the sale date. That's also why investing a little money into Edward Jones or another brokerage committed to the individualized guidance of face-to-face interactions proves wiser than going at it alone. I use CRNA Todd Zetts of Blu Dot Financial. Along with my business professor brother, I'm having him proofread this chapter, but any mistakes leading you to abject poverty are my own, not theirs. Actually, let's go a step farther and place all the blame on you.

This isn't based on any research, but I think precious metals can be considered part of an emergency savings account, as long as you also have money saved up in a non-retirement investment account. That way you can sell a stable mutual fund or stock if the market is doing well when you need cash, or a gold coin if it's faltering. But, the clear inverse relationship between the two asset classes has failed over the last few years, and you'll get better rates selling gold and silver back to the dealer than at your local pawn shop. As of this writing, it's not clear if cryptocurrencies behave as digital gold, but the easiest way to gain exposure to both worlds may eventually be Heleum. One reason that Bitcoin and physical gold preserves wealth is their difficulty of acquisition and safe storage. Neither is subject to the inflation that erodes currency and makes pennies only profitable for the endoscopist removing them from the esophagus of small children. Heleum is completely new and unproven, but it adds crypto (and eventually platinum and other precious metals) to currency trading without the multiple steps it takes to buy and safeguard investments in a physical or digital vault. Make wealth preservation fun—within reason. For both Lending Club and Heleum, I'm starting to realize that "proprietary algorithm" simply means that someone wrote unique, trendy computer code that might not work very well. Hopefully, Heleum 2.0 will fare better now that it's live.

Creating Wealth

So, preserving wealth is much more difficult if fees, insurance, taxes, and the time it takes to keep everything organized bleeds you dry (alphabetizing my Nintendo cartridges, for example). I have tried all of the methods I recommend, although spreading yourself out so thin isn't ideal. I get my jollies out of saving and investing instead of spending and having nice things. If you're not similar, a good choice might be Fundrise, because spending the 10% dividend rather than reinvesting it like a good boy or girl will feel like a nice reward. Money invested is semi-liquid. It can be withdrawn several times a year for emergencies without severe penalties, but isn't available to immediately spend on a new coat for the pug. Listen, he looks pudgy enough already, don't shame him with a poofy jacket. Even if you don't need more diversification into real estate as

Fundrise supplies, it's a good example of what to look for: profitable, overlooked markets. Others may notice how lucrative it is, but barriers to entry prevent access. In this specific case, they carefully and sustainably target apartment complexes and corporate real estate too small for the stock market volatility associated with REITs, but too large for local real estate groups on Meetup.

Like the previous example of individual high yield bonds (bond funds behave differently), I hesitate to talk about what's hot right now in late December, 2017. We can have a rational financial discussion, or we can discuss Bitcoin. The attraction to digital currencies on a blockchain is, in my own words, technology allowing observable math algorithms to fairly solve problems and logistics that currently require subjective (or corrupt) and expensive bureaucracy. Cryptocurrencies are a great way to lose all your money effortlessly, or they could save you from crushing debt. It's a completely nutty idea for those living on student loans rather than trying to avoid them, but you might as well learn how to do it right if you're going to invest. Moon shots such as this should be less than 10% of your portfolio, but the right one might change your life. Financial freedom allows you to walk away from a bad company, or at least make a job's hourly rate only one factor out of many. Let's say you're comfortable in bed, watching a new show on Netflix, and it's boring. No big deal, right? You reach for the remote–and realize it's across the room. Trapped. Now this is serious. It's the same with your current job. A tolerable work culture becomes much less so if no other options exist.

There is no better way to make other people rich (like the state lotto) than to lurch desperately into an investment. There's always time to see if the food taster keels over before the king bites into a limited-time-only steak. Buying one of the top ten cryptos and holding it is risky enough without following every hot tip, initial coin offering, or website promising to double your money if you act today. Except for books I've written and companies I own, I don't have official or unofficial affiliation with any resources or cryptocurrency I discuss. This sort of disclaimer is standard for discussions about stocks, but virtually non-existent in the haphazard world of the blockchain, with new coins to tackle real and imagined problems appearing quicker than a child can spend tokens at Chuck E Cheese. Especially for students, the key is not diversification beyond the few coins offered on Coinbase in exchange for American dollars, but simplification despite limited investment dollars. The technology is evolving so quickly that last month's recommendations are already dated and obsolete. To store value and still increase exponentially once hype fades, a coin needs real purpose and scarcity–Stellar and Ripple are compelling platforms with clear uses, but the presence of billions of coins can impact potential returns in the short term. Although partnerships with large companies drives up prices, remember that corporations benefit from the hype too, so often the emperor has no clothes.

In real estate, selling a house because the market is hot but turning around and buying another one in the same area negates some of your profit, since the second house is also expensive. It's not too different than selling a house in a depressed region and getting a good deal on another house. To profit the most by exchanging one digital coin or token for another, the goal is to sell at a peak for a cryptocurrency bottoming out. How do you do that? Making a profit in cryptocurrency is similar to booking a flight. To get to most places from Pensacola, I need to first fly to a hub. The more flights that are available (volume), the more reassured I am that price fluctuations point to an actual trend. The difference is that the hubs to reach obscure cities have the tickers BTC and ETH instead of ATL and LAX. Coins that provide new infrastructure—payment options in developing countries, liquidity for marijuana or other businesses with complex regulation—those will revolutionize fintech and survive hype bubbles. The increased adoption of cryptocurrency or the inevitability of "the next big thing" and regulation will affect the price, but let me walk through a hypothetical purchase for those interested in nanocap coins. Especially for this 2019 update, I don't think you should stray away from Coinbase or Bittrex for your needs. The blockchain is here to stay, but the top coins will continue to shift places.

After sending Coinbase all sorts of info to confirm your identity and waiting a week for your bank to clear the first transaction, purchase however much Litecoin $100 will buy. To trade it for a lesser known currency, sign up on Cryptopia and click to the Litecoin wallet address—a string of numbers and letters to copy/paste back on Coinbase and transfer the Litecoin, which is faster and cheaper than using Bitcoin to trade. Rather than trading for another coin right away, set email alerts on Coinwink.com and wait for the value of Litecoin to increase and/or the cost of one of your desired coins to decrease. Once the trade goes through, reverse it for another profit, perhaps converting the coin to Dogecoin this time for even smaller transaction fees (pennies instead of the $5 you'd expect from trading stocks.) You make real money once you cash in your tokens and leave, as you would at a casino after realizing you are lucky, not skilled. Whether utility tokens (in particular those used by "hubs" in our above example) prove to be a safer bet with various regulating bodies compared to coins designed to grow in value remains to be seen. The government doesn't consider Bitcoin or Ethereum to be securities (stocks), but not many other coins are likely to be grandfathered in. Large amounts of cryptocurrencies should be stored offline in a digital wallet, as many of the crashes in Bitcoin price are from the realization that a decentralized currency means your chance of getting money back after a mistake or breach is similar to restoring $100 bills after burning them to make a summer camp's worth of s'mores.

A discussion about making money wouldn't be complete without at least mentioning the stock market. Cryptocurrencies and private investments continue to gain ground as the way companies grow, compared to Apple and Microsoft joining the stock market as tiny companies and passing on enormous profits to shareholders for the last few decades. Similar to the hurdles to easily trading cryptocurrencies today, buying stock wasn't possible with just a few swipes of a tablet. If you're interested in any of the high risk investments I've mentioned, please make your retirement and stock picks as boring as possible. Covered calls are a possibility, but you'll have to Google it, because you'll fall asleep if I explain the concept here. The unique ability for a CRNA to work overtime or another job at a high pay rate makes it easier to recover from investment losses, but as we learned in the first part of the relationship chapter, working harder, not smarter, leads to frustration and pain.

Find obscure markets easily with ETFs. As an example, one of the funds that Fidelity offers free trades on is IFGL, a passive index of international real estate. Much easier than finding a shady website claiming to let you invest into that space directly, right? The quest for diversity shouldn't drive you to spread your money between wise and foolish investments, however. Another way to invest is to buy the stock of strong, stable companies with products you enjoy. When the stock does well, sell some of your profits.

When it does poorly, buy more. You can't go wrong doing that in a favorable market, but one of Warren Buffet's best quotes is, "You only find out who's swimming naked when the tide goes out."

Swimming Against the Tide

When do active investing and entrepreneurship come to play? The first concept to understand is the liquidity and velocity of money. The economy stagnates if money doesn't exchange hands. Transactions create capital. A balancing act ensues because money often makes more money if locked up in retirement or life insurance accounts, or the equity in your home. Getting that money out unscathed is as likely as a nurse wearing a hat and brooch teaching you best practice with the new electronic charting system. The comparison between paying or receiving 5% interest still holds true, but many companies fail because they couldn't access money they needed today. Showing up to work and collecting a paycheck every two weeks provides stability, even if you earn much more for your company that they pay you. Many small business owners survive because a military pension, spouse with a steady job, annuity, or regular dividends bridge them through a month with low sales (or, in healthcare, a month when the insurance companies delay payment to meet some internal quota of theirs). Especially if doing so without a loan, starting your own practice requires saving up that six months to a year of liquid assets.

What if you aren't creating and preserving wealth just for the American dream of the white picket fence and 2.5 children to pass it down to? As health insurance costs increase, single practitioners have a distinct advantage over those with children (or spouses with expensive hobbies, but let's not go there). Healthshare (the only one I know much about is Christian Healthcare Ministries) is a much better solution than hoping herbs and supplements will heal that femur fracture. Shopping for self-pay options and enrolling into concierge practices improves quality of life for some individuals, and from experience I can tell you that running a cash only business is much easier than dealing with the complexities of insurance. Insurance companies will screw you over when possible. Give them as little money as necessary until that fateful day. The second part of preparing yourself for full-time locums or travel nursing is debt management. Expensive car and house payments will restrict the required nimbleness of being your own boss. For a traveling job, an RV trailer is ideal—that way, if your engine blows, you still have a house, and if your house needs repairs, you still have a vehicle. I tried to link an Instagram I follow about a traveling nurse anesthetist and her tiny house, but I ended up on one featuring tiny dinosaur toys fighting.

I'm basically saying to pick exquisite furniture and other nice things, or freedom. Work hard for thirty years and retire once your wrist hurts every time you turn a stopcock, or pursue a life of semi-retirement today. Of course it's not that easy, and I still enjoy my job, so working for more years but taking time off when I want to doesn't sound frightening compared to retiring in twenty years and hoping the whole 401K thing works out. It's an individual decision to compare a nice house in a safe neighborhood to a smaller apartment but working as a 1099 contractor for an anesthesia agency in order to take every summer off. Way back in Chapter 1, I suggested taking inventory of how much prestige, learning opportunities, salary, and flexibility matter to you. Contract work isn't flexible if you have to jump at every possibility because the bills have to be paid.

Choosing between austerity and luxury has a third option, the venerable side hustle. We've already touched on this a few times, mainly to state that making money from hobbies should never distract from the actual healthcare job that pays bills. In the context of financial freedom, try AirBnb to rent out part of the house, or all of it while you're away. Conversely, renting instead of buying a chainsaw or kayak prevents the accumulation of rarely used stuff that prevents most of us from taking the whole month of August off like those lucky Europeans. The gig economy falls apart quickly if there's no enjoyment from helping people write essays on fivver.com or meeting new people by driving Uber or HyreCar. Remember that no one is making you keep up with the Joneses, or lose an hour every day on your commute from an exclusive suburb's HOA, or buy alcohol at restaurants and tip 22%. Don't bother being your own boss until you set the financial rules of what brings you joy and closer to others in your spending and saving.

Never quite having enough cramps generosity. At the onset of the Great Depression, churches opened their doors to the poor as they always had as a social safety net in American society. Unfortunately, that didn't last long. The excesses of the Roaring

Twenties infected places of worship, and they still had mortgages to pay on their ornate new buildings. You'll spend wiser if it's not all going to you. Spending 10% of your income on self development isn't a substitute for charitable giving, but also reaps rewards beyond the money sewn into counseling, massage, classes, etc. Self improvement fine tunes self promotion to attenuate the awkwardness. Perhaps you've written a book as I have and realized that charming self-deprecation certainly doesn't work in anesthesia ("it'd be great if you trusted me with your life, but giving medicine is more of a hobby, really), so neither should it for anything else you're willing to commit both time and effort. If someone is excited about one of my many side projects, I invite them to my play or show them where to buy my book. But, the cold calling approach of "It never hurts to ask" makes me shift you from the category of "friend doing cool things" to "person who thinks I'm a sucker and wants to sell me stuff."

Earlier, I said that the ability to allocate assets to where they're needed is more important than interest rates or the total amount of money. Start a business, but realize that entrepreneurship is often a combination of doing what you love, what makes money, and what you fear. Respectively, those ingredients provide passion, sustainability, and, most importantly, the challenge to stretch and overcome. Innovate through fear to set your business apart from those without the nimbleness, personal touch, trustworthiness, or other unique facet that only you offer. Perhaps I should say, "What makes you hesitate" instead, because fear also makes every job a great deal harder than it needs to be, whether that manifests in relationship struggles, showing up an hour early for clinicals, or letting inflation erode the value of cash while waiting for a riskless and foolproof investment opportunity (or, to be fair, insisting that any company that uses the word "blockchain" take all your money).

The ideal business structure may vary, but I recommend getting a good accountant or learning on your own rather than relying on Legalzoom or similar services to charge you for supplying the forms an Internet search could have revealed. Especially if starting small—which depending on the practice may be wiser than a highly visible launch while still figuring out the basics—it's easier to delegate jobs such as bookkeeping if a rudimentary knowledge already exists. Otherwise, the bar is set for a good accountant to just be someone who keeps you out of jail and is cheaper than another random accountant. Forming an LLC in your state and requesting the IRS to tax the business as an S Corporation tends to balance legal protection with simplicity fairly well. The same brokerages offering college savings options have solo 401K options or Simplified Employee Pension (SEP) plans.

Resources

White Coat Investor covers student loans, life insurance options, wills, stocks, and a host of other financial issues for medical professionals. Along with the aforementioned Bludot, they provide charts to calculate the best solutions for your situation. Give every dollar a job and budget in real time instead of after the fact with YNAB. Similar to relationships, all the love and resolve in the world won't matter without sustainable habits to make determination reality. For those still struggling with debt, Dave Ramsey offers principles to add discipline and take more emotion out of your spending and saving. Jon Acuff combines humor and wisdom flawlessly for speakers, authors, and entrepreneurs. For advance practice nurses, I'm active in a CRNA business and Bitcoin Facebook group.

Speaking of Bitcoin, earn a few cents daily while accumulating all of the Bitcoin forks (similar to dividends) with Qoinpro. The website doesn't support Ethereum, so myetherwallet.com and equivalent paper or digital wallets are safer choices for most coins. Because cryptocurrency is at least as risky as private company investments, the posts on earlyinvesting.com explain both types of investments very well. Hybrid, SEC approved combinations of equity crowdfunding and initial coin offerings list on StartEngine and Republic.co. The ETF BLOK provides exposure to these technologies without the volatility. I try to concentrate on one alternative investment yearly, although I use mint.com to track all of my diverse holdings. Even if investing is a fun hobby, it takes too much time to track the best deals on comparegoldprices.com and visit seedinvest.com every day in hopes of finding a new metal or company to invest in.

We've journeyed to the second of three endings in this book, as nurses wanting more information about anesthesia school are encouraged to keep reading the appendix. Hopefully, you've improved the skill of taking textbook knowledge and applying it to individual patients. My desire for relationships and finances is to fill your hearts with new ideas more than crowding more content into your minds. In each case, we transform abstract information into something to personally use and own. That's the secret to sustainability. Tweak it until it is an integral part of who you are. Some of us have to loosen up and break our poverty mindsets of scarcity so others can give themselves to us fully and we can occasionally, dare I say it, splurge on ourselves instead of getting our kicks from hoarding every penny (or emotion). Others are realizing the need to sacrifice for others—delaying gratification now for richer fulfillment later. Wherever you are on your journey, you will succeed. Life might not play out as envisioned, but flexibility and refusing to wallow in contempt or self-pity allows happiness and fulfillment to find you. It may be an ambush of joy or a slow, inconsistent process. As you live in the present and cherish that moment, gratitude emerges and takes root deep in your soul. Godspeed.

About the Author

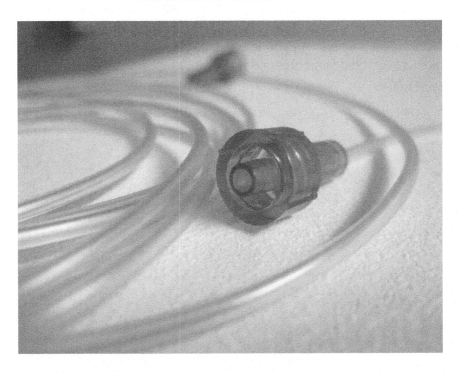

Find more books by Nick Angelis at Amazon or other retailers. Feel free to snicker at his slovenly excuse of a Twitter (@DrippingEther) Instagram (@EtherDripper) and Youtube, or send him hate mail and delicious spam at his AOL address, Bloogooroo.

You can also subscribe to the author's updates at BEHAVEwellness.com, an organization committed to the war against workplace bullying. Ok, maybe it's not a full-fledged war, but it should certainly be a substantial conversation rather than a topic more neglected than the short and spindly kids in PE class. Similar to other forms of abuse, hazed and harassed students replicate those behaviors onto the next generation of learners. The result is a corrosive environment that decreases learning while increasing cost, in part because of limited productivity. Taking the maximum amount of sick days, moving from job to job, and working part time are all common situations for the targets of abuse. Thankfully, Mr. Angelis is a full time (plus lots of overtime) Certified Registered Nurse Anesthetist in northeast Ohio and northwest Florida when he is not when he is not planning the launch of Alleviant Health Centers Akron or actively pestering his acquaintances and coworkers to buy this book and his other titles, all published by GG Press.

GG Press is a subsidiary of the alternative medicine company that brought you *The Grecian Garden: A Natural Path to Wellness*, mentioned several times in this book as the premier research driven project about natural health that still manages to be conversational, accurate, and practical. Blah blah blah—wait, you've entered the hidden BONUS section! What, right here, right now?! Yes, starting with the audio version of this book to listen to or download at http://archive.org/details/howtosucceedinanesthesiaschool.

I am discarding the third person voice that better allows for self-aggrandizing to introduce two anesthesia-related stories from my satire storybook *The Twerk Vaccine*. You may want to skip around a bit—although useful or fun, everything from here on isn't universally applicable, or I would have written it in 2012 for the first version of this book. It's also more specific to anesthesia—more similar to the invaluable role of remifentanil for a select niche of patients rather than the Dilaudid that everyone enjoys. After a brief foray into the world of medical satire, our glorious journey will end with my sharing of some tidbits, shreds, and poorly formatted scraps of disorganized rough draft ramblings from a collaborative project for prospective CRNAs I'm working on. I called it the appendix because it is dangling at the end of the book and we're not sure why it's there (not because it's filled with waste and needs to be cut out.) It's so secretive I'm not even going to tell you the name of the book or second author until we're closer to publishing in, uh, 2020, probably.

Curare Darts Phased out Despite Drug Shortages

Macon, Georgia: Like many medical centers, St. Joseph the Protector Hospital is experiencing severe drug shortages, especially in the operating room (OR). The latest unobtainable drug is the non-depolarizing paralyzing agent Succinylcholine, usually reserved in surgery for rapid sequence intubation of the trachea. The search for an acceptable alternative began with St. Joe's newest surgeon, Dr. Lawrence, suggesting the immortal properties of cobra venom.

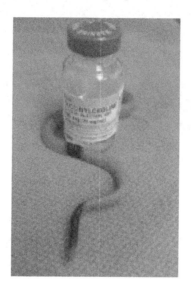

"I sent the nurse anesthesia students to the medical library to examine the literature for a safe, preferably natural substitute," said chief nurse anesthetist Agatha Gudell. "They returned with a Google search on curare and a blow gun from the nearest pawn shop."

In direct contrast to computerized charting, this novel approach increased efficiency while decreasing cost, but anesthesiologist Dr. Glide has ordered a new protocol for paralysis once the current supply of curare darts is exhausted. "We would shoot the patients in pre-op and they would be very quiet and relaxed before surgery— none of that annoying chattiness Versed sometimes causes. Despite increased compliance and apparent serenity, our patient satisfaction scores have plummeted."

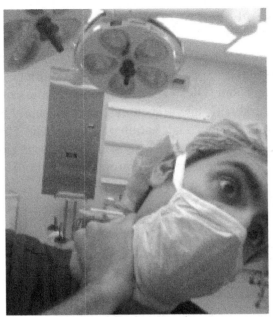
Aim has also been an issue.

Dr. Glide's solution? With curare and most other substances derived from rainforest plants now on backorder, the South American manufacturer revealed they can provide the anesthesia department with either Succinylcholine at greatly inflated prices or a bargain poison arrow frog shipment canceled by Zoo Atlanta.

"The patients will love it," assured Mrs. Gudell. "We'll sedate them adequately before requesting they lick a frog in the OR. Those with larger tongues, who might otherwise be more difficult intubations, will naturally cover more frog surface area with a lick, so we don't even have to use math and calculate dosages for adequate muscle relaxation. Best of all, if the patients lick a frog twice, Dr. Foster will finally get the complete paralysis he demands for skin closure." Mrs. Gudell immediately paged the nurse anesthesia students to send reports of this new finding to both *Anesthesia & Analgesia* and *Nature*, but upon further investigation, the students were found marching around the OR with hair dryers awkwardly tucked into their scrub pants. One of them shrugged apologetically.

"We're out of Robinul to dry patient's secretions."

Editor's Note: No animals or humans were permanently harmed while reporting on this story, but one reporter still remains intubated after trying to pet a colorful frog.

Spare Anesthesia Machine Makes Slushies

Sante Fe, New Mexico: Dr. Brad Jacks suspected it for months. Anesthesia personnel would leave for a break in the middle of a quick ear tubes procedure and come back to the OR room fifteen minutes later, clutching their heads and whimpering about "brain freeze."

"The worst is anesthesiologist Darrell Cameron," stated Dr. Jacks. "You can't trust someone with two first names, and after he takes a break the patients always wake up sputtering because of his constant dripping tears from these mysterious headaches. Even more mysteriously, his suction makes all these horrible noises, like he's clearing secretions from Jabba the Hut."

Dr. Cameron was not available to interview due to a schedule conflict with a scheduled break, but we did catch up with nurse anesthetist Rusty Shawn. He initially ignored our questions, steering the conversation toward less newsworthy topics, such as the pronunciation of his last name (past participle of the word see). He denied all allegations until this astute reporter noticed a creamy blue raspberry slushie in Rusty's non-intubating hand.

Can you identify the six flavors mentioned in this article?

"It's true," Rusty murmured sheepishly. "We bribed someone from the Biomed department to help us build it right in our break room. Everyone else thought it was a backup ventilator, and against JCHO regulations, we never even allowed the maintenance guys to inspect it! We've been able to keep our slushie machine a secret for so long because even suspicious Dr. Jacks didn't dare turn the lever to nitrous oxide or isoflurane—but those flavors are actually blueberry and grape!"

Rusty's face darkened. "It would still be a secret, too—our lovely, icy, refreshing, sugary secret, if Dr. Cameron hadn't been too jittery from his favorite lemon banana slushie. Every alarm on his anesthesia machine made him jump, so he substituted our slushie machine in its place. I don't know what he was thinking, but that hungry little patient of his was so happy when Dr. Cameron pushed the oxygen flush button and green apple slushie came out!"

Appendix: Secret Scholastic 'Sthesia for Student Nurses

What is a CRNA

It's important to first describe what a Certified Registered Nurse Anesthetist (CRNA) does all day. That way, if none of the following glamorous details are of interest, you can shut this book and spare yourself some enthralling but unnecessary reading. Some readers are already anesthesia students and won't need this refresher—go intubate someone, we're done here. Not all depictions of this line of work are complimentary. In the entertainment world, CRNA's are occasionally displayed accurately as the providers most often inserting epidurals (usually before the birth of nefarious alien or vampire spawn). However, in many TV shows, books, and movies, anesthesia personnel are lucky to get a split second cameo tapping a bag of IV fluid or similarly memorable tasks. This is the same amount of attention a CRNA might want in real life. It's a job similar to a soccer goalie: no one pays much attention unless you mess up.

Contrary to the operating room persona of working behind the scenes, CRNA personalities tend to be anything but invisible. The road from a bachelor-prepared nurse in the Intensive Care Unit (ICU) to a CRNA with at least a master's degree is a long one. It takes a strong personality to stand up to surgeons when necessary, and a peculiar one to enjoy meticulously controlling the vital signs of anesthetized patients every day. That's not to say that healthcare career choices should be based on certain attributes. Dull and boring personalities can be just as successful as sparkling ones, so there's no need to resign yourself to squinting at bacteria as a pathologist or working for a plastic surgeon because you resemble an "after" picture. For students, there are certainly traits and attitudes that will increase the chance at success, but we'll discuss those in the appropriate chapters.

For a typical CRNA, the day starts in the preoperative area where the first nervous patient awaits. For healthier patients undergoing minor procedures, a quick clinical examination coupled with questions about every organ system is all that is required—similar to a yearly physical but with an airway exam and more detailed questions about prior surgeries and anesthetics.

Patients and surgeries entailing more risk require extensive testing beforehand. Electrolyte imbalances must be corrected and blood cell counts and clotting ability adequate for the procedure. Planning for the "worse-case scenario" always involves placing intravenous access sufficient to administer blood products if needed and sometimes invasive monitors for arterial and venous pressures. If the patient has heart disease, part of the preoperative work-up can include acquiring an EKG, cardiac echo, stress test results, and clearance from a cardiologist.

After seeing the patient, the anesthetist gathers the necessary drugs and equipment, based upon the preoperative assessment. Drug shortages, cost, efficiency, and the availability of a good crosswords puzzle are important variables. Well, not the puzzle, but anesthesia truly requires personalized care. A drug perfect for stabilizing the vital signs in one patient could easily harm the next patient. Just to put a patient to sleep, five different drugs may be used at individualized doses, with several other drugs prepared for emergencies and to keep the heart rate and blood pressure at reasonable levels.

Equipment preparation includes testing the anesthesia machine. Mouth-to-mouth resuscitation is a decidedly "old school" response to an anesthesia circuit leak in most circles, so check that $50,000 piece of machinery thoroughly! We'll give a more detailed overview of necessary preparations later. Once the surgeon has seen the patient, the CRNA often graciously augments empathy and reassurance with calming pharmaceuticals before the patient travels to the OR.

The next five minutes tend to be the most exciting of the day. Once monitors are attached, the patient is quickly anesthetized, paralyzed, intubated with an endotracheal tube, and positioned securely for surgery. Depending on the vital signs, the CRNA may give more anesthetic gas, narcotics, or other medications to adjust blood pressure and other variables. This process continues throughout the surgery, but toward the end of the case, the CRNA adjusts the ventilator, anesthetic gas, and any infusions to slowly wean the patient off the ventilator and wake them up. After a successful extubation, the patient is merrily transported to the recovery room. Once the CRNA is satisfied with the patient's condition, the process begins again. There you have it. That's all we do. Over and over again. The process is slightly different for sedation cases, and epidurals, spinals, regional nerve blocks, and invasive line placement are other important CRNA tasks, but most of it happens in the OR or the units immediately adjacent. It's a narrow, highly specialized field that doesn't easily lend itself to a "second career" the way a frustrated ICU nurse can go start her own home health care company. As a certain unemployed cardiologist in California can attest, home health anesthesia works poorly—yes, I just went there. If it's any consolation, few highly specific and sought-after skills do transfer easily, unless your name is Bo Jackson or Charlie Ward. I suppose our potential readership will drop significantly if we explain all of our stupendous conclusions with sports analogies, so an alternative example would be the dismal failure that greets most movie actresses who attempt to also become singing sensations.

Of course, it would be easier to acquire the skill set of a CRNA if you already had those characteristics, right? Not necessarily—I chose nurse anesthesia in part because I hated math, unaware that I would be converting drugs dosages into micrograms per kilogram per milliliter just about every day. Also, I am laid back and a current member of First City Improv because making up life as I go along comes naturally to me. I don't match the rigid personalities around me. This same skill set is only a six week course in dentistry, after all. Realize that you need to train for the worst that could happen, which rarely involves getting a tooth pulled at the dentist. This is the heart of the matter: much of our work can be confidently accomplished by an anesthesia student finishing a second or third semester of clinical work. Suddenly, a patient can't be ventilated or unexpectedly flatlines. Immediately, the CRNA must take quick, decisive action to save the patient's life. Oh, and it has to be the correct action, too. Cases such as the above or a patient suddenly moving while under the knife require reflexive decisions followed by more thorough analysis. In other instances, careful consideration of a problem's root cause takes precedence over courageously emptying the contents of the drug tray into the patient. As an older CRNA used to say, "The most important drug in those drawers is the tincture of time."

Not everyone in anesthesia will agree on the best course of action for a given situation. If the esteemed authors of this book simultaneously anesthetized identical twins for identical procedures, the end result would be similar, but the exact drugs, dosages, and clinical decisions could vary considerably. A mishap not attributable to the patient, surgeon, or equipment malfunction would be the only way to gauge which method proved superior. This is why we're writing a book about anesthesia school instead of a glossy, tri-fold pamphlet with fun pictures and bright colors.

In lieu of those pretty pictures, let's simplify the conversation for a moment, especially since some of you may be new to healthcare and may already be confused by our hypnotic prose. Entry level jobs in healthcare perform specific tasks at the direction of nurses or other team members who are responsible for "critical thinking." To avoid receiving letters about the virtues of various "aid" and "tech" jobs, we will refrain from giving specific examples. Part of making wise, informed decisions is knowing how to solve problems yourself and when to call the person above you. Nurses carry out physician orders for treatments and medications and serve as a safety check to make sure the patient receives appropriate interventions. The nurse's assessment skills to gauge patient response are increasingly augmented by more detailed and complex monitors in the intensive care units. There, nurses also have the ability to titrate intravenous infusions to keep patients stable as they learn valuable experience from working closely with one or two critically sick patients.

This is why working in an intensive care unit is mandatory before anesthesia school, so that a candidate can more easily transition into the acuity of care and drastic changes in patient condition that are the reality of life in the OR. To compare it with other healthcare settings, let us use the useless analogy of meals, primarily because my stomach just growled as I typed this sentence. If patient units are the sit-down restaurants in the continuum of healthcare, the OR resembles a frantic fast food joint, with perhaps a nursing home on the other side of that continuum represented by a patient pot roast (as in the virtue, not the person needing health services). Obviously, this pace is impractical twenty-four hours a day, so even large trauma centers need fewer workers in the OR than your local Wal-Mart does at midnight.

One advantage over floor nursing is that anesthetists rarely have to work weekends and holidays, since few patients would enjoy waking up on a Saturday or Christmas morning to have surgery. Not being a morning person, my personal philosophy is, "I don't care if they beat me every day, as long as the beatings don't start until seven am." If you're balding, it could be years before your coworkers notice, thanks to surgical hats. By the same token, it could take a while to find an opportunity to wear that lovely dress because you'll be in scrubs all day. Parading around in a favorite outfit before clocking in is rarely as subtle as OR and anesthesia personnel think it is. Besides the morning parade, what are OR people really like? They enjoy a quick pace, a juicy story, and the adrenaline thrill that comes with life in the surgical suite. Everything is faster, whether it's the speed of infusions or the time it takes a doctor to go from mild irritation to spectacular fury.

Before you cross the threshold into the OR, we will need to spend some time on successfully navigating that volatile culture. However, more daunting for potential candidates are the vast stores of knowledge needed to succeed in anesthesia. We need to understand every interaction a patient's home medicines could have with our drugs. For many students, even this pales in comparison to the task of transforming that knowledge into something clinically useful for a wide variety of surgeries and procedures. The technical skills of a baccalaureate nurse are often limited to the catheterization of various veins and orifices. These skills are most important in the emergency department setting but rarely used in a sub-acute facility. Ironically, career advancement requires expertise in a new array of technical skills, not just the learning of more in-depth pharmacology and physiology.

Performing nerve blocks or tracheal intubation incorrectly have much more serious consequences than an orderly misjudging bedpan placement. The relatively high salary of a CRNA reflects the responsibility owed to those entrusted in their care. The CRNA must decide on the medications and interventions that will result in the safest care of the patient. This is harder than it would seem, as the most conservative options may not be the easiest or the most comfortable for the patient. Despite high liability, in other cases a more "risky" approach may be the best choice for a specific patient. An example would be a cystoscopy. Many patients find the concept of a metal scope inside their bladder disturbing, so the CRNA can sedate them with intravenous drugs, render them unconscious via anesthetic gas from a mask, laryngeal mask airway (LMA), or endotracheal tube, or allow them to enjoy the experience awake and pain free after an epidural or spinal anesthetic.

Of course, the typical CRNA doesn't offer each of those detailed choices to a patient. After we evaluate the patient, we consider the surgeon preferences as well before we adequately inform the patient of their options. A CRNA is still a nurse, with the ability to communicate with patients, physicians and everyone in-between as an advocate for best practices and patient safety. Our most important skill set still lies between our ears as we make the important decisions that keep patients pain-free and asking, "When are we going to start the procedure?" as we transport them to the recovery room.

Technology

The year was 2004. I stared at the thick monitor screen laying horizontal on the nurses station. This would revolutionize health care and simplify electronic health records! A device this portable would be as convenient as a paper chart while granting nurses the ability to easily access information on all their patients. Unfortunately, technology didn't progress as I envisioned, and despite the evolution of the tablet since I first saw that prototype, today most hospitals consider laptops chained to a rolling desk the ultimate blend of technology and convenience.

Brace yourselves, for this is the section where we will discuss the expensive technology imperative to your anesthesia education. Let me tell you, I'd be killing patients left and right if it wasn't for my iPad, weekly simulation exercises, and $400 dollar a year software subscriptions. Just kidding, you don't need any of that. Save your money for food and for clothing without drawstrings and awkward pockets that tempt you to wear a fanny pack (which would be useful to house all sorts of technological clinical adjuncts if you ignore my upcoming advice). Besides, everyone suspects that an anesthetist with a fanny pack is just hoarding all the super special drugs like Nimbex and whatever the hospital ran out of this week.

It is important as an anesthesia student to desperately cling to anything that will give you an edge in clinicals, whether that be cryptic notes from previous students or that little handbook that usually has answers about every situation except the one you're

135

facing. So, I'm not saying to ignore all the nifty little gadgets out there, though I'd prefer you ignore my dated colloquialisms.

The first step is to visit the library. On campus, this place is often inhabited by studious types much brighter than you. It's much easier to research a paper or find obscure answers to unfair clinical questions with institutional access to CINAHL and similar databases. "Obscure" is key as I've only used CINAHL a handful of times when Google and Wikipedia failed me. I mean, the references at the bottom of a Wikipedia article, of course. The quality of research you'll need is much higher in graduate school. A vague disease description from WebMD or similar lay person health site will prove completely worthless. Don't lie, you've probably read that website and thought, "Wow, that describes my awkward symptoms entirely!".

Another problem quickly emerges when standard search engines find spectacular research articles on that genetic disorder only affecting Ethiopian immigrants settling in the outer suburbs of Los Angeles. The abstract doesn't sufficiently answer your questions, and accessing the full article costs money. This is the point where you tearfully ask a librarian for help or access one of the simpler medical databases, all of which have applications for mobile devices. Continually squinting at .pdf files on a three inch screen is a poor choice, but so is running to the campus library every time you need information that a dozen anesthesia textbooks forgot to discuss. I'm not asking every adult learner to retool the way they learn or study to appear trendy. There are certainly advantages to having a physical book or anesthesia journal in your hands, but the more portable you can be, the better. Textbooks are always cheaper in an e-book format, and at some clinical sites you won't get a locker or even a hook on the wall to hang a book bag.

It's easier to clean blood off your phone case in the OR than it is to disinfect your laptop. Besides, medical libraries are more likely to have free access to downloadable clinical apps for Android, Blackberry, Microsoft, and iOS devices than your university will. For you young'uns, Blackberry is like an iPhone with a real keyboard and your choice of about ten apps. Anyway, many of the practical clinical tools such as Micromedex aren't always available in academia. The key is to find one or two sources for acquiring research articles and clinical tools and stick with them.

You'll find that the librarians in a hospital library will be able to help you tremendously, but don't wear out your welcome by asking them to find every article on rabies written since the death of Pasteur. Whether you are at a clinical site for a few weeks or working as a nurse at a hospital, assume that your badge is all you need to access library services. This is especially important since medical libraries are the best hiding spot since the invention of the linen closet. How many times have you heard people say, "Well, I have all the education I need for my profession, but I think I'll try to find the library during my lunch break and do some reading." For the most part, your only companions will be sleepy medical students surreptitiously making copies and sipping caffeinated beverages. Just remember that this hiding place is only for situations where there is nothing useful to do at a clinical site. You may already suspect that appearing lazy and unmotivated will give you a reputation only slightly better than seeming homicidal and incontinent.

The best program and application I've found is MDConsult. It has been replaced with Elsevier, which isn't quite as user friendly. After you sign up at a hospital, it works from any internet connection with a simple username and password, even if you leave that institution. Access will eventually expire, which is only fair. At that point you will have to register through your current clinical site's library to continue the service. Talk to your medical librarian to see what kind of access you can obtain that allows you to search through a variety of medical, allied health, and social science journals, even though some articles will only have abstracts available. Searches can be expanded to textbooks, including full volumes of Miller's Anesthesia. After a full day of anesthesia clinicals and an hour long nap, I spent many a night working as a nurse in the ICU reading those monstrous volumes from a computer screen.

Reading hard to understand textbooks won't work if you're multi-tasking. That kind of distraction is detrimental to patient care, which is why I could only do it under certain conditions. Especially as a student, absolute vigilance is a necessity. Our culture's inability to focus on a singular task must be unlearned in anesthesia school.

We'll speak more of this in other sections, but the relevance of avoiding distractions is very important when discussing apps and mobile devices. The days of clunky PDAs only offering solitaire and a calculator for entertainment are long gone. From a distance, the frantic finger movements required for an IV calculation app may be confused with those needed to crush candy, or green pigs with infuriated fowl.

As previously stated, these devices are not a requirement. If you already have a smart phone, the process of adding a few free clinical tools is fairly streamlined. Instead of investing in an unlimited data plan, simply use the hospital's internet servers. Call the help desk for assistance if needed. There's a pattern here of getting help from varied hospital departments that normally don't cross paths with each other or with the anesthesia department, no matter how small the hospital. Regardless of how kind and willing to help the anesthetists may appear, ask for their assistance only when you can't obtain answers from people who won't be evaluating your clinical performance (and by extension, every facet of your abilities and personality).

Of course, the hospital's tech help desk and library won't be able to tell you specifically which free anesthesia application is best for iPad or an Android smart phone. This is where your classmates and former students come in, and the increasingly vital "CRNAs and SRNAs" Facebook group. The only one I use is Anesthesiologist. A good app will also serve as a study guide and link to drug calculations and information (usually through Epocrates) rather than require you to use several programs at once. Many newer drugs such as Precedex have their own free apps. Just use whatever mobile device you already have; an expensive tablet is not going to give you an edge on other students. Search for key words in the major app stores that work with your device and keep in mind that apps exist for blood gas calculations and other laboratory data, anatomy, and even cardiac clearance. You may want to trial specific apps if you have a specialty rotation for a month, but remember that figuring out computer programs could be a lengthy process.

What should you do if you don't have a smart phone or tablet but really think one would be useful clinically? I've cut this informative paragraph out of the paperback version, because it's a waste of paper and ink. Your grandma has a smart phone. If you don't, perhaps I'll publish this information on a papyrus scroll hidden inside a clay pot just for you, shipped exclusively by Amazon. I know that my cell phones are usually not working very well by the time my two-year contracts are due to renew, even if I haven't dropped them more than twice a day.

My current phone barely has the technology to text, but my

younger brother came to my rescue. His old phone won't work as a replacement if his new one breaks, because the battery only lasts a few hours. He gave me his old phone as part of a birthday present, which was still better than the trading cards from the 1992 election that I gave him, even though he got the much coveted AIDS card.

I took his phone to work and put it in airplane mode to conserve battery life since the call function is now useless. The phone can still connect via Wi-Fi. The camera on the phone also allows me to use it as a cheap scanner to email myself documents, study guides, or whatever else I need stored electronically. I'm not saying you need to abandon your cell phone and save money by only taking Skype or Google calls on a tablet (though I did consider that in school, and it's a clever way to call your phone and find it). Rather, don't carry around useless products that only serve to poorly replicate technology you already have access to. You're already squinting at vocal cords all day long, so why bother trying to read you're your smart watch? Checking email or using a copy machine is rarely a problem, while I have yet to see a hospital with a color scanner or Snapchat account.

Speaking of social media, don't post anything from the hospital or the university on it (unless it's on Friendster, Myspace, or some other long discarded site), and don't "friend" any superiors until you graduate. You'll have so little privacy as it is, so why add more situations where you need to think carefully before you speak? I still have a strict no-physician-friends-on-Facebook policy. If that's a problem for you, consider not downloading social media applications on a device used for school, or don't access those apps at clinical sites. I realize that I'm highlighting only the cheapest options for you to become technologically proficient in the OR; for more expensive choices, go buy the $100 equivalent to this book and tell me what you learn.

Your anesthesia school may decide to purchase expensive software for documenting all the wonderful experiences to be had in clinical rotations. Although time consuming, this method is less prone to error than cutting a notch in your scrubs drawstrings every time you intubate a patient, or cutting a corner off your nurse's hat every time you miss an IV. It may prove difficult at times to know when I am being serious, but I assure you that this is not one of those times. Just like many of the better healthcare apps, the advantage is the ability to input and output data whenever connected to the internet.

One of my major points of this chapter is to demonstrate ways to make your education and studying portable and seamless, so that you can use every spare moment to study, document clinical experiences, and learn without being obvious or rude about it. Just remember to be aware of how your behavior may be interpreted. During clinicals, burying your nose in a textbook appears more studious than playing with your mobile device. On the other hand, I boldly brought pocket-sized textbooks to funerals, weddings, and other important social occasions where a cell phone would have been more discreet.

There is one more area of technology that will differ widely from program to program. Any good nursing program will have medical mannequins for nervous students to attempt IVs, bladder catheterizations, nasogastric tube placement, and all the other horrible things nurses do to awake patients every day. The term "simulation lab" runs the gamut from cheap models you might suspect were stolen from the local mall to complex clinical situations featuring mannequins run by computer algorithms. However, correctly accessing a mannequin's trachea or epidural space is much different than a patient's. I always tell students, "You can't become an expert at parallel parking by driving on the freeway."

My venerable co-author has strong arguments against the excessive use of simulations instead of real patients, so I tried to find a CRNA with a differing opinion. The idea is not to purposely make this book controversial but to avoid watering down insights for the sake of moderation. Start reading about nitrous oxide in an anesthesia textbook and you'll quickly understand the uselessness of summarizing polarizing viewpoints. You'll find references about nitrous oxide for the exact same uses with phrases like "may be useful" *and* "may prove detrimental".

I suspect that providing opposing points of view will be of more value to readers than a middle-of-the-road approach tempered with reason (and boredom). My brother develops military simulations for billion dollar fighter jets, and the comparison to anesthesia simulations is a simple one offered by our colleague. Mary Williams, CRNA, MSN is author of the handy clinical guide *Simply Anesthesia* and a faculty member of Lourdes University Program of Nurse Anesthesia.

"Pilots are required to re-visit the simulator training program once every six months where they are given real life scenarios to manage. This training, required throughout their career, reinforces their actions in a crisis, making them almost rote. Simulation training is more important than forty Continuing Education Units (CEUs) every other year and repeated 'tests' to validate a CRNA's knowledge. Programs with simulation training are important in the development of competent CRNAs. If the student is allowed to practice scenarios multiple times, mistakes are made in the simulation lab and not in the OR. This has been proven in research involving ACLS (Advanced Critical Life Support) and BLS (Basic Life Support) simulation training courses, not only pilot training."

Application Process: Screening

Most anesthesia schools require candidates to take the Graduate Record Examination (GRE) or similar generic screening exams. If you have a screen door, bugs can't get in because they're not equipped or smart enough to open it. Please don't think that the real reason is because they're too big to fit through the holes, or you'll ruin my example. In the same way, the GRE and Graduate Management Admissions Test (GMAT) screen out those whose academic expertise outside the field of nursing is lacking.

Increased specialization makes it difficult to learn completely different concepts. That's why the pulmonologist thought I was crazy for recommending probiotics for my elderly relative with recurrent pneumonia: she was just focused on the lungs in isolation. Perhaps this is why anesthesia school candidates tend to score around the fiftieth percentile on the GRE. I intend to offhandedly discuss my score at some point in this paragraph if I can contrive a way to do so without appearing smug and pompous. At any rate, the GRE was last significantly updated in 2011, so study materials before that date may be less useful. However, I would still start with typical library resources before doing anything rash like paying for tutors or the latest test seminar. The Quantitative Reasoning portion is still algebra and geometry, and Pythagoras has yet to release a modern edition to his cursed theorem.

The other two sections of the test are Verbal Reasoning and Analytical Writing, which collectively ensure that graduate school candidates can read and write. Practice tests will help you understand the style of questions and correct answers likely appearing in Verbal Reasoning, and the most concise ways to articulate the points of view in the Analytical Writing section. I use the word "concise" because the latter section allots you a mere thirty minutes to logically argue a point of view and an additional thirty minutes to pick apart someone else's argument on a different topic.

What if you're not a good test taker? Remember that your attitude and state of mind makes a huge difference. Your sympathetic nervous system does wonders for your athletic abilities but poops out fairly quickly in a test environment. That's why Pythagoras didn't make his triangular breakthrough until he retired from his Olympic boxing career. Lies about my Greek ancestors aside, practice calming and focusing techniques. Recent advances in neurology and psychology have unveiled the wisdom in training the brain how to better retain and recall information—LearningRx is an example if there is a franchise in your area. It's similar to the tortuous weeks of conditioning I endured at the beginning of soccer season before the coach would allow us to start kicking balls at each other. Skills don't help without the stamina to sustain them. Although anesthesia students sometimes resort to methods from Adderall to alcohol, there are some supplements that can help you focus. Referring you to the natural health resource mentioned earlier is one way to do justice to this topic, as only a holistic and thorough approach that includes emotional aspects of learning will make a difference. Personally, I frame tests in the context of a competitive challenge to prove how smart I am. Consider staring at a computer screen in a room full of nervous test takers as an adventure or game instead of an expensive way to potentially prove your incompetence. That way, a twinge of nervousness interpreted as excitement isn't as difficult to channel into focus on each individual question.

On the opposite spectrum of anesthesia school requirements lies the enigmatic goal of acquiring the "right" nursing experience. At minimum, the nurse must spend a year in an intensive care unit (ICU) to master taking care of artificially ventilated patients with invasive lines and powerful vasoactive infusions. Some nurses take to the ICU like a penguin to water, while others struggle like a penguin in flight. Before you flap your frail flippers at me indignantly, let me state that there is nothing wrong with being a nurse for a decade before pursuing anesthesia school. Some nurses benefit from spending time in other departments, honing beneficial skills such as IV placement that are harder to come by in the ICU.

I started a job at the most revered ICU within five hundred miles before the ink dried on my diploma. I quickly realized that working for only a few months before applying to anesthesia school was not the ideal road for me and that my scholastic achievements were irrelevant clinically. I was hoping to follow that sentence with an explanation comparing my academic prowess to a swimming penguin tearing apart a leopard seal, but it's time to let that analogy ice over and discuss the pros and cons of specific nursing units.

Medical ICUs often feature the most complex patients because of the multiple effects of organ dysfunction. Worst case scenario, organ systems crumble into chaos as the patient's family members frantically try to make up for lost time as their loved one slowly dies. Did I mention that nursing requires a strong sense of empathy and ethics? Anyway, because they are in a state of chronic deterioration, MICU patients tend to have fewer Swanz-Ganz catheters and other invasive monitors than surgical and trauma ICU patients. Much like information about Halothane for anesthesia boards, some experience with interpreting data from these invasive monitors is a must for anesthesia school, if only for historical purposes. The bodies of the chronically ill find innovative ways to adapt, so laboratory and other test results careen past "abnormal" to land on "ridiculous".

SICU and cardiovascular ICUs are prime areas for ambitious candidates to receive their obligatory experience before launching to anesthesia school. Even if the patients were in good health prior to surgery, acuity changes second by second. Nurses often receive the new patient report from CRNAs after surgery and gain valuable experience with common anesthetic agents as the patient recovers from anesthesia. A disadvantage of these units is that some of the finer parts of nursing skill are more difficult to learn among the frenetic pace and abundance of monitors and infusion protocols that can limit true critical thinking.

Cardiac and neuro ICUs are alternative places to work before anesthesia school, each with their own unique pharmacological and interventional therapies. However, it is a slightly harder sell if the candidate only has experience in those medical units. Specialization in thrombolytic agents or the latest anti-seizure drugs is of limited use in general surgery, as is knowledge limited to pediatric ICUs. Every nursing job provides valuable insight into patient management that should translate into anesthesia care. Of course, the only way to experience all of these units is to become an agency nurse (fulfilling a role similar to a substitute teacher) or join the hospital float pool.

Rather than a literal pool where nurses and penguins frolic about, this term refers to floating from unit to unit wherever there is a need. A typical nursing shift on a medical or surgical floor can require the nurse to care for ten patients who wouldn't look out of place in the aforementioned MICU. The difference is that these patients don't have quite as many monitors and readily available doctors to assist the nurse in discerning fluid, electrolyte, or other imbalances. Also, prioritizing care for so many patients inevitably results in some tasks remaining unfinished. The emergency department (ED) is another place where prioritizing acuity is paramount. The added benefit in the ED is the variety of patient conditions and interventions that the nurse quickly learns, from placing nasogastric tubes and large bore IVs to participating in codes.

I've worked many shifts in all of the above specialties and more, but I don't have any personal experience as a procedural or operating room (OR) nurse or as a recovery room nurse. Although inadequate for critical care experience, these environments do help potential anesthesia students learn the way the strange world of the OR works. That's the whole reason nursing experience is so critical for anesthesia school. Communication with other professionals and the ability to self-evaluate is invaluable. You'll meet a lot of jerks in high acuity areas, so feel free to use the resources available at BEHAVEwellness.com to avoid being bullied or distracted from your ultimate goal. Use as many parts of your brain and learn all the skills and experience you can to ease that transition from a nurse following orders to a CRNA administering therapies and pharmacological interventions.

Evaluating Available Programs

Selecting a potential anesthesia school is a daunting task. Accurately comparing cost, prerequisites, and expected workload among different schools is next to impossible, whether you rely on Google, the AANA, or just vicious local rumors as a primary resource. The hospital I was born in and later worked at has a mural on the cafeteria wall almost as distasteful as the food. It features a local map and the words "Bloom Where You're Planted," a slogan deeply ingrained in nursing culture. All else being equal, the closest anesthesia school should always be your first choice, even without considering the cost savings of in-state tuition. Unless you hate the weather, your family, and your local elected officials, it makes sense to learn anesthesia near your community. Anesthesia students often become CRNAs at their former clinical facilities. Think of it as an unpaid internship, except even more demeaning. Since even the more devoted students tend not to enjoy the drudgery of anesthesia school, the most important facet of the decision making process is the quality of a program.

Quality of the Program

Quality and prestige are not necessarily synonymous. The adequacy of a nurse anesthesia education is not measured by the awards won by a clinical director or a pretty building and simulation lab. Our aforementioned proponent of simulation labs, Marie Williams, CRNA, MSN, has a distinct opinion on a quality education.

"A program with a variety of clinical sites, including multiple sites with CRNA only practices is critical to really developing the full spectrum of clinical skills that students and CRNAs need to be well-rounded practitioners. It is not enough to be trained to be part of an anesthesia care team model with an MDA monitoring or 'overseeing' your practice. The fully trained CRNA must be fully independent and crisis ready."

By that definition, higher quality programs may be in states with fewer medical supervision requirements and in underserved, rural areas where CRNAs are the only anesthesia experts. This is the opposite approach to pursuing the big city "brand name" hospitals and universities world renowned for their academic prowess and clinical breakthroughs. Those institutions provide cutting edge experiences for the anesthesia student, but at the price of less autonomy. From that flashy world of the newest research and techniques and oldest and sickest patients comes the perspective of Dave Godden, CRNA, MSN, writer of the blog www.nurseanesthetist.org.

"Personally, I want a national or even an internationally known alma mater and am willing to pay the slight difference in cost. From an economic standpoint, you have to include travel and relocation into that formula. Not all of us live within a short drive of USC or Georgetown."

A small school can't offer you the newest and most innovative research, tools, and surgeries found at a large academic institution. A large school is less likely to expose you to the self-reliant experience of a nurse anesthetist in smaller institutions. So, if you've always dreamed of practicing in the heart of New York City, a tiny program in Iowa might not be the best fit.

In my experience, the presence or absence of anesthesiologists at a clinical site is a minor issue. The hospital's culture matters much more: are students encouraged to master new techniques, or are they quickly reprimanded for imperfection? I experimented with countless techniques and drugs at laid back hospitals and concentrated on consistency and reproducibility at uptight clinical sites. Obviously, those details can't be extrapolated from an interview or tour of the OR. "Diploma mills" bent on accepting tuition from as many students as possible may err on the side of graduating inadequately trained CRNA's, while a program with too tight a hold on its students may graduate emotional wrecks with a limited experience base due to fear of failure. I'm talking about central line placement and nerve blocks, as there's often a long line of medical residents and nurse anesthetists who want those experiences. Students are more marketable if they have extensive training in these rarer skills, but for simpler tasks, having 2,000 intubations instead of 1,000 just means you were overworked and had less time to prepare for boards than other students.

All of this talk of finding a program representative of the perfect bowl of porridge may prove useless if you're more of a Simple Simon than a Goldilocks. Programs with a good reputation from previous graduates snap up the more qualified students. If you simply aren't the best candidate or have been denied twice by other schools, you may end up at an overpriced or lower quality institution. Most of your clinical skills will be honed one on one with a CRNA, regardless of where you train. Your attitude will determine how much you can learn from each person. Work on your ability to communicate effectively; as an added benefit, it will improve your innate skills at avoiding evil preceptors. It's not a simple task because many of the strictest CRNA's are also the ones most dedicated to helping students really learn anesthesia.

Finally, relax. Fear and anxiety leads to procrastination (and irregular bowel habits). Just like preparing for boards and other important exams is easier in the context of a game or competitive challenge, so is the arduous process of selecting an anesthesia school. This is an exciting chapter in your life. Your knowledge and ability to care for patients will increase exponentially as you learn impressive skills that will soon triple your income. As with any success story not involving lottery tickets, hard but satisfying work comes before the payoff.

Word of Mouth

In healthcare, the difference between a rumor and an expert opinion is blurry at best. The gold standard for dispersing information seems to be word of mouth. One reason is that the authority structure of most hospitals is more complex and updated more frequently than the algorithms for ACLS. I can attest that at my hospital it looks like Joseph Smith and Bringham Young's family trees. I'm sorry, that was inappropriate. The administrators who make policy decisions rarely cross paths with those in direct patient care. Separate disciplines barely have time to talk to each other, let alone other providers.

Of course, hearsay about layoffs or new standards and protocols isn't the only unverified information bantered about. The standard for what's acceptable personal information to share about people is lower than in other occupations. We shed tears and sweat with our coworkers, and patients shed much grosser fluids and solids with us. When one of my coworker is pregnant, conversation quickly turns from how many months along she is to how dilated her cervix is or the extent of her constipation.

All this is magnified in the close quarters of the OR, especially the speed of traveling stories. As he took out a gallbladder yesterday, a surgeon told us he might retire next month. Seconds later, another nurse anesthetist appeared to offer me a break. I walked into the break room to hear a staff member say, "That's too bad that he'll be gone after next month."

The obvious lesson here is to keep your mouth shut, but the second is that sometimes you have to use rumors. A study claiming you can cure leukemia with the tail of a petulant wombat would be ignored unless two other studies showed similar results. In the same way, if several people warn you against a hospital or school, you should take heed to their complaints.

We can use these concepts to better understand healthcare culture in general. It's a rigid world where respect initially depends on the initials following the name on your ID badge. A charismatic bed side manner works to achieve a patient's devotion, but lasting respect from other providers depends on clinical and critical thinking skills. We all have a list of which surgeon, anesthetist, nurse, etc. we'd prefer to take care of us if we ever had the misfortune of being a patient. Poise, confidence, and a gracious, hard-working attitude isn't enough if you make poor decisions or can't reliably manage a patient's airway.

To further complicate matters, doing what you're told isn't always the best way to stay out of trouble because of the concept of "patient advocacy." This means that you should always do what's right for the patient, regardless of protocol or procedure. Someone, probably a nurse with a clipboard but less education and experience than you, wrote a protocol, perhaps as a reflex because of something bad that happened to an individual patient. Your patient is someone completely different, and it's your judgment to see if the protocol applies. For example, I eagerly depleted my ICU's saltine cracker stores until one tragic day when a sign appeared with the dreaded words "Nourishment for Patients Only". After a few months of abstinence, patients started sputtering on the now stale crackers. If they were well enough to eat a cracker, patients were shipped out of the ICU, so the cracker stores were not being replenished. The only noble option was to start raiding the cracker cabinet again.

I hoped you paused after reading that last paragraph to reflect on the limitless sacrifices I endure for the betterment of the sick and infirmed. As a student, placing patients before procedures may be limited to politely pointing out solutions that you think would improve patient care. The alternative of ignoring the advice of the clinician precepting you never works out well, although it differs among professions. Fearful of impending legal liability and because of our training, nurses tend to chart copiously and conform to the "letter of the law". In some cases, this leads to using practical, evidence based practice less often than we really should considering the problem solving the job requires. This is a hard habit to break in anesthesia, where individualized care means that some patients will need three or four times more medication or a novel approach to achieve a safe and pleasant outcome. The trend, especially as nurse practitioners and similar clinicians expand their scope of practice, is to standardize care, but this rarely works out well for the substandard patient.

Let me close this section out with a useless analogy from the last movie I saw. Wisely, health care and anesthesia culture admires the Spock approach: cautious, conservative, consistent, and humble. I apologize if you were hoping for a fourth adjective starting with the letter "c". There are rare situations where the best outcome for the patient is an approach more reminiscent of Captain James T. Kirk's courageous decisions, but that method usually results in intergalactic criminals crashing into San Francisco. That's also why paramedics and nurse anesthetists seem to have similar skill sets but are actually worlds apart.

THE END

No, really, that's all I've got, so go study already.

64479898R00086

Made in the USA
Middletown, DE
29 August 2019